Quantum Machine Learning with Qiskit and TensorFlow Quantum

Combining Quantum Computing and Deep Learning Techniques to Solve Complex Problems in AI and Data Science for the Next Era of Computing

Greyson Chesterfield

1

COPYRIGHT

DISCLAIMER

This book is designed to provide information. Every effort has been made to make this book as complete and accurate as possible, but no warranty or fitness is implied. The information is provided on an "as is" basis. The author and the publisher shall have neither liability nor responsibility to any person or entity with respect to any loss or damages arising from the information contained in this book or from the use of the programs accompanying it. This book contains examples of code and techniques that are provided for instructional purposes. While the author has made every attempt to ensure the accuracy and quality of the code, it should not be used as-is in professional or production environments without thorough testing and verification. The views expressed in this book are those of the author and do not necessarily reflect the views of any company or organization.

13

Chapter 1: Introduction to Quantum Machine Learning

Overview of Quantum Computing

Quantum computing represents a revolutionary leap in computational capabilities, harnessing the principles of quantum mechanics to process information in fundamentally different ways compared to classical computers. At its core, quantum computing utilizes quantum bits, or qubits, which can exist in multiple states simultaneously due to the property of superposition. This ability allows quantum computers to perform complex calculations at speeds unattainable by classical computers, especially for problems involving large datasets or intricate optimization tasks.

In classical computing, data is processed in bits that are either 0 or 1. In contrast, qubits can represent 0, 1, or any quantum superposition of these states, exponentially increasing the amount of information that can be processed. Furthermore, qubits can be entangled, meaning the state of one qubit is intrinsically linked to the state of another, regardless of the distance between them. This unique feature of entanglement enables quantum computers to solve certain problems more efficiently than their classical counterparts.

The development of quantum computing has the potential to revolutionize a variety of fields, including cryptography, materials science, and artificial intelligence (AI). Quantum algorithms, such as Shor's algorithm for factoring large numbers and Grover's algorithm for searching unsorted databases, demonstrate that quantum computers can outperform classical computers in specific applications. As the technology matures, researchers are increasingly exploring how quantum computing can enhance machine learning processes, leading to the emergence of quantum machine learning.

Emergence of Quantum Machine Learning (QML)

Quantum Machine Learning (QML) is an interdisciplinary field that merges quantum computing and machine learning, aiming to leverage the power of quantum algorithms to improve the performance and efficiency of machine learning tasks. This area of research has gained significant traction in recent years due to the exponential growth of data and the limitations of classical machine learning techniques in handling such complexity.

The intersection of quantum computing and machine learning is rooted in the recognition that many machine learning problems, such as optimization, pattern recognition, and data classification, could benefit from the enhanced computational capabilities offered by quantum systems. For instance, classical machine learning algorithms often struggle with high-dimensional data and complex feature spaces, leading to long training times and suboptimal solutions. Quantum algorithms, on the other hand, have the potential to perform these tasks more efficiently, allowing for faster training and more accurate models.

QML can be broadly categorized into two main areas: quantum-enhanced classical algorithms and quantum algorithms specifically designed for machine learning tasks. Quantum-enhanced classical algorithms utilize quantum computing to speed up certain aspects of classical machine learning processes, such as data encoding and optimization. Quantum-specific algorithms, such as quantum neural networks and quantum support vector machines, are designed from the ground up to exploit quantum mechanics for learning from data.

As researchers continue to explore the capabilities of QML, early applications have already shown promising results in various domains, including drug discovery, finance, and image recognition. These advancements suggest that QML may lead to breakthroughs in AI and data science, providing tools to tackle complex problems that were previously intractable with classical methods.

Importance of QML in AI and Data Science

The importance of Quantum Machine Learning in the broader context of AI and data science cannot be overstated. As data generation accelerates and the complexity of data increases, the demand for more powerful computational tools becomes urgent. QML offers several compelling advantages that position it as a critical component in the next generation of AI technologies.

One of the most significant benefits of QML is its ability to process vast amounts of data quickly. Quantum computers can exploit the principles of superposition and entanglement to perform many calculations simultaneously, which is particularly advantageous for tasks such as data classification, clustering, and regression. This capability allows researchers and practitioners to develop models that can learn from large datasets more efficiently, reducing the time required for training while improving model accuracy.

Moreover, QML has the potential to overcome the limitations of classical algorithms, particularly in scenarios involving high-dimensional data. Classical machine learning models often rely on assumptions that may not hold in high-dimensional spaces, leading to issues such as the "curse of dimensionality." Quantum algorithms, however, can navigate these complex spaces more effectively, enabling the discovery of patterns and relationships that may be obscured in classical frameworks.

Another area where QML can make a significant impact is in optimization problems. Many machine learning tasks, such as hyperparameter tuning and model selection, involve finding optimal solutions in large search spaces. Quantum optimization algorithms, such as the Quantum Approximate Optimization Algorithm (QAOA), offer the potential for exponential speedup in solving these problems, allowing for more sophisticated models to be trained in less time.

Furthermore, the integration of quantum computing into AI raises intriguing possibilities for new types of learning models that capitalize on quantum phenomena. Quantum neural networks, for example, utilize quantum circuits to process information, potentially leading to novel approaches in deep learning. As researchers continue to experiment with these concepts, we may see the emergence of entirely new paradigms for understanding and leveraging data.

As the field of QML evolves, it is also important to consider the societal implications of this technology. The ability to analyze and interpret large datasets with unprecedented speed and accuracy raises ethical questions regarding data privacy, security, and the potential for bias in algorithmic decision-making. Researchers must prioritize ethical considerations in the development of QML algorithms to ensure that the technology is used responsibly and equitably.

Goals and Structure of the Book

This book aims to provide a comprehensive exploration of Quantum Machine Learning, focusing on the practical application of quantum computing techniques using tools like Qiskit and TensorFlow Quantum. As the field of QML continues to develop, it is essential for practitioners and researchers to gain a solid understanding of both the theoretical foundations and practical implementations of these concepts.

The structure of the book is designed to guide readers through the essential elements of QML, starting with the fundamental principles of quantum computing and machine learning. Each chapter will delve into specific topics, providing in-depth coverage of both the underlying theory and hands-on tutorials for implementing QML techniques using Qiskit and TensorFlow Quantum.

In the following chapters, readers will explore the fundamentals of quantum computing, the basics of classical machine learning, and the ways in which these two fields intersect. Subsequent chapters will focus on key QML concepts, including quantum data representation, quantum neural networks, quantum kernel methods, and training quantum models. Practical applications of QML in various industries will also be examined, highlighting the real-world impact of these technologies.

Additionally, the book will address the challenges and limitations associated with QML, as well as ethical considerations and future trends in the field. By providing a balanced view of the opportunities and challenges within QML, this book aims to equip readers with the knowledge and tools necessary to navigate this rapidly evolving landscape.

As we embark on this exploration of Quantum Machine Learning, readers are encouraged to engage with the material actively. Practical exercises, case studies, and real-world applications will be included throughout the book to reinforce learning and demonstrate the potential of QML in solving complex problems. The integration of hands-on tutorials with theoretical discussions will enable readers to develop their skills and apply their knowledge in meaningful ways.

In summary, this introductory chapter has set the stage for the exploration of Quantum Machine Learning, outlining the fundamental principles, the significance of QML in AI and data science, and the goals of the book. With this foundation established, readers are prepared to delve deeper into the fascinating world of quantum computing and its intersection with machine learning in the chapters that follow.

Chapter 2: Fundamentals of Quantum Computing

Basics of Quantum Mechanics

Quantum mechanics is the branch of physics that deals with the behavior of matter and energy at the atomic and subatomic levels. Unlike classical physics, which is governed by deterministic laws, quantum mechanics introduces a probabilistic framework where the outcomes of measurements can only be predicted in terms of probabilities. This fundamental shift in understanding has profound implications for the development of quantum computing.

At the heart of quantum mechanics is the concept of the quantum state, which describes the complete information about a quantum system. Quantum states can be represented mathematically using vectors in a complex vector space, known as Hilbert space. One of the most striking features of quantum states is superposition, a principle that allows a quantum system to exist in multiple states simultaneously. For example, a qubit can represent both 0 and 1 at the same time, which is a key aspect that enables quantum computing to perform multiple calculations concurrently.

Another crucial concept in quantum mechanics is entanglement. When two or more qubits become entangled, the state of one qubit becomes dependent on the state of another, regardless of the distance separating them. This phenomenon can lead to correlations that are stronger than those allowed by classical physics, enabling quantum computers to perform complex computations that classical computers cannot efficiently achieve.

Measurement in quantum mechanics introduces another layer of complexity. When a quantum system is measured, it "collapses" to one of its possible states, and the probabilities associated with the superposition determine the likelihood of each outcome. This inherent uncertainty and the non-local nature of quantum entanglement challenge classical notions of information and computation, paving the way for new computational paradigms.

Quantum Bits (Qubits) vs. Classical Bits

Classical bits, the fundamental units of information in classical computing, can exist in one of two states: 0 or 1. In contrast, qubits are the fundamental units of information in quantum computing and possess unique properties that enable quantum computation. A qubit can represent not only the states 0 and 1 but also a superposition of both states, which is mathematically represented as:

$|\psi\rangle = \alpha|0\rangle + \beta|1\rangle$

Here, $|\psi\rangle$ represents the state of the qubit, while α and β are complex numbers that determine the probabilities of measuring the qubit in state 0 or state 1, respectively. The absolute squares of these coefficients ($|\alpha|^2$ and $|\beta|^2$) give the probabilities of obtaining each state upon measurement, and the constraint $|\alpha|^2 + |\beta|^2 = 1$ ensures that the total probability remains normalized.

The ability to be in a superposition of states enables qubits to perform parallel computations, a property that gives quantum computers their potential advantage over classical computers. When multiple qubits are used, their combined states can represent an exponentially larger amount of information. For example, n qubits can represent 2^n possible states simultaneously, allowing quantum computers to explore many solutions to a problem in parallel.

However, working with qubits also introduces challenges. Quantum states are fragile and susceptible to decoherence, where interactions with the environment cause loss of information. Maintaining the coherence of qubits while performing computations is one of the primary challenges in the development of practical quantum computers.

Quantum Gates and Circuits

Quantum gates are the building blocks of quantum circuits, analogous to classical logic gates in traditional computing. While classical gates manipulate bits in fixed ways (e.g., AND, OR, NOT), quantum gates operate on qubits and exploit the principles of quantum mechanics to perform transformations on quantum states.

Quantum gates can be represented using unitary matrices, which are mathematical constructs that preserve the inner product of quantum states. For example, the Hadamard gate (H) creates superposition by transforming a qubit state $|0\rangle$ into a state where it has equal probabilities of being measured as 0 or 1:

$$H|0\rangle = \frac{1}{\sqrt{2}}(|0\rangle + |1\rangle)$$

Other common quantum gates include the Pauli-X gate, which acts like a classical NOT gate, and the controlled-NOT (CNOT) gate, which creates entanglement between two qubits. The CNOT gate flips the state of a target qubit if a control qubit is in state 1:

$$\text{CNOT}(|00\rangle) = |00\rangle, \quad \text{CNOT}(|01\rangle) = |01\rangle, \quad \text{CNOT}(|10\rangle) = |11\rangle, \quad \text{CNOT}(|11\rangle) = |10\rangle$$

Quantum circuits are constructed by combining these gates in specific sequences to perform computations. The design of quantum circuits requires careful consideration of gate arrangements, as the order of operations affects the final output due to the non-commutative nature of quantum operations.

Quantum circuits can be visualized as directed acyclic graphs, with qubits represented as lines and gates as nodes connecting these lines. A typical quantum circuit begins with qubits initialized in a known state, followed by a series of quantum gate applications, and concludes with a measurement that collapses the quantum state into a classical output.

The power of quantum circuits lies in their ability to create complex superpositions and entanglements that enable efficient computation for certain problems. As researchers develop quantum algorithms, they aim to design circuits that maximize these quantum phenomena, leveraging the unique capabilities of quantum mechanics to outperform classical algorithms.

Superposition, Entanglement, and Measurement

Superposition, entanglement, and measurement are fundamental concepts that differentiate quantum computing from classical computing and underlie the advantages of quantum algorithms.

Superposition allows quantum systems to exist in multiple states at once, enabling parallelism in computation. This property is crucial for algorithms that require the exploration of large search spaces or the simultaneous evaluation of multiple solutions. For instance, Grover's algorithm leverages superposition to search an unsorted database quadratically faster than any classical algorithm by evaluating many possibilities at once.

Entanglement further enhances the computational power of quantum systems. When qubits are entangled, the measurement of one qubit instantaneously affects the state of another, regardless of the distance between them. This non-local correlation can be harnessed for quantum communication protocols, such as quantum teleportation and superdense coding, as well as for developing quantum algorithms that exploit the interconnectedness of qubits.

Measurement in quantum mechanics is the process of extracting information from a quantum system. Upon measurement, a quantum state collapses to one of its possible eigenstates, with probabilities defined by the state's coefficients. This process introduces inherent uncertainty, as the outcome cannot be determined precisely until the measurement is made. The act of measurement plays a crucial role in quantum computing, as it transforms quantum information into classical information, allowing us to interpret the results of quantum computations.

In summary, understanding these fundamental concepts of quantum mechanics is essential for grasping how quantum computing operates and why it holds the potential to revolutionize various fields, including machine learning and artificial intelligence. The unique properties of qubits, coupled with the principles of superposition, entanglement, and measurement, provide a powerful framework for developing new computational paradigms that challenge traditional approaches. As we move forward in this book, these principles will serve as the foundation for exploring the intricate relationship between quantum computing and machine learning.

Chapter 3: Introduction to Machine Learning

Overview of Classical Machine Learning

Machine learning (ML) is a subset of artificial intelligence (AI) that focuses on the development of algorithms and statistical models that enable computers to perform specific tasks without explicit programming. Instead of following rigid instructions, ML systems learn from data and improve their performance over time. The growth of digital data has catalyzed the rise of machine learning, as vast amounts of information can now be analyzed to extract meaningful patterns and insights.

Classical machine learning can be broadly categorized into three main types: supervised learning, unsupervised learning, and reinforcement learning. Each of these paradigms serves different purposes and is suited for various applications, reflecting the diversity of tasks that machine learning can address.

In supervised learning, the model is trained on a labeled dataset, where each input is paired with its corresponding output. The goal is to learn a mapping from inputs to outputs so that the model can predict the output for new, unseen data. This approach is widely used in applications such as image recognition, speech recognition, and predictive analytics. Popular algorithms in this category include linear regression, decision trees, support vector machines, and neural networks.

Unsupervised learning, on the other hand, deals with unlabeled data. The objective here is to discover hidden patterns or groupings within the data without prior knowledge of the outcomes. Common techniques include clustering algorithms, such as k-means and hierarchical clustering, and dimensionality reduction methods, like principal component analysis (PCA). Unsupervised learning is often used in exploratory data analysis, customer segmentation, and anomaly detection.

Reinforcement learning represents a different approach, where an agent learns to make decisions by interacting with an environment. The agent receives feedback in the form of rewards or penalties based on its actions, and its objective is to maximize cumulative rewards over time. This paradigm has been successfully applied in various domains, including robotics, game playing, and autonomous systems. Algorithms such as Q-learning and deep reinforcement learning have gained prominence in recent years due to their ability to handle complex environments.

The increasing complexity of data, combined with the limitations of classical algorithms in handling high-dimensional spaces, has prompted researchers to explore new computational paradigms. As traditional machine learning approaches face challenges in scalability and efficiency, the intersection of machine learning and quantum computing offers promising avenues for improvement.

Key Concepts: Supervised, Unsupervised, and Reinforcement Learning

Supervised Learning

Supervised learning is one of the most widely used paradigms in machine learning. It involves training a model on a labeled dataset, where the algorithm learns to map inputs to known outputs. The process begins with the collection of data, which is then split into training and testing sets. The model is trained on the training set, adjusting its parameters to minimize the error in predicting the outputs. Once the training is complete, the model's performance is evaluated on the testing set to assess its ability to generalize to new, unseen data.

Common algorithms used in supervised learning include:

Linear Regression: This algorithm models the relationship between input features and a continuous output variable by fitting a linear equation. It is often used for predicting numerical values, such as housing prices or stock prices.

Decision Trees: Decision trees are hierarchical structures that recursively split the input space based on feature values, leading to decisions at the leaves of the tree. They are intuitive and can be easily visualized, making them popular for classification tasks.

Support Vector Machines (SVM): SVMs are powerful classifiers that find the optimal hyperplane separating different classes in the feature space. They are particularly effective in high-dimensional spaces and are often used for text classification and image recognition.

Neural Networks: Neural networks consist of interconnected layers of nodes (neurons) that learn to extract features from data through backpropagation. They have gained prominence in recent years due to their success in deep learning applications.

Supervised learning is highly effective when labeled data is abundant, but it requires significant effort in data annotation and may struggle with overfitting if the model is too complex.

Unsupervised Learning

Unsupervised learning involves training models on data without labeled outputs. The primary objective is to identify patterns or structures within the data. This approach is particularly useful when the true underlying structure is unknown, or when labeled data is scarce.

Key techniques in unsupervised learning include:

Clustering: Clustering algorithms group similar data points together based on their features. Common clustering methods include k-means, which partitions data into k clusters based on proximity, and hierarchical clustering, which creates a tree-like structure of clusters.

Dimensionality Reduction: Dimensionality reduction techniques aim to reduce the number of features while preserving essential information. Principal component analysis (PCA) is a widely used method that transforms data into a lower-dimensional space by identifying the directions of maximum variance.

Anomaly Detection: Anomaly detection focuses on identifying unusual patterns that do not conform to expected behavior. This approach is valuable in fraud detection, network security, and fault detection.

Unsupervised learning is particularly advantageous for exploratory data analysis, allowing researchers to uncover hidden patterns and insights that may not be immediately apparent. However, it can be more challenging to evaluate the performance of unsupervised models, as there are no explicit labels to guide the learning process.

Reinforcement Learning

Reinforcement learning (RL) is a unique paradigm where an agent learns to make decisions through interactions with an environment. The agent takes actions, receives feedback in the form of rewards or penalties, and adjusts its strategy to maximize cumulative rewards over time. This approach is particularly useful for tasks involving sequential decision-making, where the consequences of actions may not be immediately apparent.

Key concepts in reinforcement learning include:

Agent: The learner or decision-maker that interacts with the environment to take actions.
Environment: The context in which the agent operates, including the state space and reward structure.
Reward: A scalar feedback signal received after taking an action, indicating the success or failure of that action.
Policy: A strategy employed by the agent to determine its actions based on the current state.
Value Function: A function that estimates the expected return (cumulative reward) from a given state or action.

Common reinforcement learning algorithms include Q-learning, which learns a value function through trial-and-error, and deep reinforcement learning, which combines deep learning with reinforcement learning techniques to handle complex state spaces.

Reinforcement learning has achieved remarkable success in various applications, such as game playing (e.g., AlphaGo), robotics, and autonomous systems. However, it often requires a significant amount of data and computational resources to train effective agents.

Neural Networks and Deep Learning

Neural networks are computational models inspired by the structure and functioning of the human brain. Comprising interconnected layers of nodes (neurons), neural networks learn to represent and process data through a series of transformations. Each neuron applies a weighted sum of its inputs, followed by a non-linear activation function, to produce an output. This architecture allows neural networks to capture complex patterns and relationships in data, making them highly effective for various machine learning tasks.

Deep learning is a subfield of machine learning that focuses on using deep neural networks with many layers. These deep architectures enable the learning of hierarchical feature representations, allowing models to extract increasingly abstract features from raw data. For instance, in image recognition, early layers may learn to detect edges, while deeper layers identify more complex patterns, such as shapes or objects.

The success of deep learning has been driven by advancements in computational power, the availability of large datasets, and improved training techniques. Popular deep learning frameworks, such as TensorFlow and PyTorch, provide tools for building and training deep neural networks, making it easier for researchers and practitioners to implement complex models.

Deep learning has achieved state-of-the-art performance in various domains, including image classification, natural language processing, and speech recognition. However, it also presents challenges, such as the need for large labeled datasets and the risk of overfitting, particularly when training on small datasets.

Limitations of Classical Approaches

While classical machine learning techniques have made significant strides, they also face several limitations that can hinder their effectiveness, particularly in the context of increasingly complex data and applications.

One of the primary challenges is the curse of dimensionality. As the number of features in a dataset increases, the volume of the feature space grows exponentially, making it more difficult for classical algorithms to find meaningful patterns. This phenomenon can lead to overfitting, where models become too tailored to the training data and perform poorly on unseen data.

Additionally, classical machine learning algorithms often rely on assumptions about the underlying data distribution, which may not hold in practice. For instance, many algorithms assume that the data is linearly separable, which can limit their applicability to real-world problems with non-linear relationships.

Moreover, training classical models can be computationally intensive, especially for large datasets or complex models. As data continues to grow in size and complexity, the limitations of classical approaches become more pronounced, prompting researchers to seek alternative solutions.

In this context, the integration of quantum computing with machine learning presents a promising avenue for overcoming these challenges. Quantum algorithms have the potential to provide significant speedups for certain tasks, enabling more efficient processing of high-dimensional data and the discovery of patterns that may be elusive to classical methods.

As we delve deeper into the world of Quantum Machine Learning, the foundational knowledge of classical machine learning will serve as a critical backdrop for understanding how quantum techniques can enhance and transform these approaches. The next chapters will explore the principles of quantum computing and their applications in the context of machine learning, laying the groundwork for a deeper exploration of Quantum Machine Learning techniques and their potential to solve complex problems in AI and data science.

Chapter 4: Quantum Data Representation

The Nature of Quantum Data

Quantum data representation refers to the encoding of classical information into quantum states, leveraging the unique properties of quantum systems to enhance data processing and analysis. Unlike classical data, which is typically structured as binary bits, quantum data is represented using qubits, enabling a richer and more complex form of information encoding. This shift opens new avenues for machine learning and artificial intelligence, as quantum data representation can harness superposition and entanglement to provide distinct advantages.

In quantum computing, data is encoded in the amplitudes and phases of quantum states. A single qubit can represent both 0 and 1 simultaneously, leading to a multitude of potential states when multiple qubits are combined. This characteristic allows for efficient representation of complex data structures. For example, a system of nnn qubits can represent $2n2^n2n$ different states at once, enabling the simultaneous processing of vast amounts of information.

The quantum representation of data must be carefully designed to exploit these properties effectively. Quantum states can be visualized using Bloch spheres, where points on the surface represent different qubit states. The use of superposition allows for multiple dimensions of data to be encoded into a single qubit, while entanglement facilitates the correlation of qubits in ways that classical bits cannot achieve.

Quantum data representation is crucial for the development of quantum algorithms that can outperform their classical counterparts. By effectively encoding data into quantum states, researchers can create algorithms that leverage the unique capabilities of quantum computing, opening new possibilities for data analysis, pattern recognition, and problem-solving.

Quantum States and Qubit Encoding

The representation of classical data as quantum states requires an understanding of how qubits can be manipulated and transformed. A qubit can be in a state of 0, 1, or a superposition of both states. Mathematically, a qubit's state is expressed as:

$|\psi\rangle = \alpha|0\rangle + \beta|1\rangle$

where $|\alpha|^2 + |\beta|^2 = 1$. Here, α and β are complex coefficients that represent the probabilities of measuring the qubit in the corresponding states upon observation.

To encode classical data into quantum states, one approach involves using basis states that correspond to specific data points. For example, in a binary classification problem, each class can be represented by a distinct qubit state. More complex data can be represented by entangled states, where the combined states of multiple qubits capture correlations among features. This enables the quantum system to represent multidimensional data efficiently.

Quantum states can also be prepared using various quantum gates. For instance, the Hadamard gate can transform a qubit from a definite state to a superposition:

$H|0\rangle = \frac{1}{\sqrt{2}}(|0\rangle + |1\rangle)$

This transformation allows classical data to be encoded in a way that takes advantage of quantum parallelism.

In addition to standard qubit encoding, there are advanced techniques such as amplitude encoding and angle encoding. Amplitude encoding allows the representation of classical data as amplitudes of a quantum state, where the coefficients of the state vector correspond to the data values. This method is particularly useful for representing high-dimensional data while keeping the qubit count relatively low.

Angle encoding involves mapping classical data into the angles of a quantum state on the Bloch sphere. This technique allows for efficient representation of data points in a format suitable for quantum algorithms, enabling the application of quantum gates to manipulate and analyze the encoded information effectively.

Quantum Data vs. Classical Data

The distinction between quantum data and classical data is essential for understanding the implications of quantum machine learning. Classical data is structured and processed using classical algorithms that operate on bits, while quantum data leverages the principles of quantum mechanics to represent and manipulate information in fundamentally different ways.

One key difference is the ability of quantum data to exist in superposition. In classical systems, a bit can only be in one of two states (0 or 1) at any given time. In contrast, a qubit can represent both states simultaneously, leading to exponential growth in the representation capacity of quantum systems. This capability allows quantum algorithms to process large datasets in parallel, significantly improving efficiency and speed.

Another significant difference lies in entanglement. While classical data operates independently, quantum data can exhibit strong correlations through entangled qubits. This interconnectedness enables quantum algorithms to exploit these relationships for more efficient processing and analysis. For example, entangled states can be used in quantum communication protocols to enhance security and data transfer rates.

Moreover, the measurement process differs fundamentally between classical and quantum data. In classical systems, data can be observed directly without altering the state of the information. In quantum systems, however, measurement causes the quantum state to collapse, introducing uncertainty. This unique aspect necessitates careful consideration in the design and implementation of quantum algorithms, as the outcome of measurements influences subsequent operations.

The advantages of quantum data representation become increasingly apparent as we explore applications in machine learning. By encoding data into quantum states, researchers can create algorithms that leverage the unique properties of quantum mechanics to tackle complex problems that are challenging for classical methods. As quantum machine learning evolves, the ability to represent and manipulate data in quantum form will be pivotal in unlocking new capabilities and improving the efficiency of AI systems.

Quantum Encoding Schemes

Quantum encoding schemes are essential for translating classical data into quantum representations suitable for processing by quantum algorithms. Various methods have been proposed to effectively encode different types of data, each with its own advantages and challenges.

Amplitude Encoding

Amplitude encoding is a popular quantum encoding scheme that allows classical data to be represented as the amplitudes of a quantum state. In this approach, a vector of classical data values is mapped to a quantum state where the amplitudes correspond to the data points. For example, a dataset with N entries can be encoded in $O(N) O(\sqrt{N}) O(N)$ qubits, as the amplitudes of the

44

quantum state can represent multiple data values simultaneously.

This method is particularly advantageous for high-dimensional datasets, as it reduces the qubit count required for representation. The trade-off, however, is that the initial preparation of the quantum state can be complex, requiring careful normalization of the data to ensure the resulting state is valid.

Angle Encoding

Angle encoding offers another effective method for representing classical data in quantum states. In this scheme, each classical data point is mapped to an angle on the Bloch sphere, allowing the qubit's state to be represented as:

$$|\psi\rangle=\cos(\theta 2)|0\rangle+\sin(\theta 2)|1\rangle|\psi\rangle = \cos\left(\frac{\theta}{2}\right)|0\rangle + \sin\left(\frac{\theta}{2}\right)|1\rangle|\psi\rangle=\cos(2\theta)|0\rangle+\sin(2\theta)|1\rangle$$

where θ corresponds to the classical value. This approach allows for the representation of continuous data in a way that can be manipulated using quantum gates.

Angle encoding is advantageous for its simplicity and compatibility with quantum algorithms, particularly in the context of quantum neural networks and quantum variational algorithms. However, it may require additional qubits for representing higher-dimensional data.

Quantum Feature Maps

Quantum feature maps are techniques used to transform classical data into a quantum representation that emphasizes relevant features. This approach involves mapping classical inputs to higher-dimensional quantum states, allowing quantum algorithms to exploit the additional information for improved performance.

A common example of a quantum feature map is the quantum kernel method, which uses quantum circuits to compute the similarity between data points in a high-dimensional feature space. By encoding classical data into quantum states and measuring the inner products of these states, quantum feature maps can facilitate advanced machine learning tasks, such as classification and regression.

These encoding schemes exemplify the diverse methods available for quantum data representation. Each approach presents its own challenges and advantages, depending on the specific application and data type. As researchers continue to explore and refine quantum encoding techniques, the potential for quantum machine learning to revolutionize data analysis and pattern recognition becomes increasingly apparent.

Implications for Quantum Machine Learning

The representation of data in quantum form carries significant implications for the field of quantum machine learning. By harnessing the unique properties of quantum states, researchers can develop algorithms that outperform classical counterparts in various applications.

One of the most notable implications is the potential for improved efficiency in data processing. Quantum algorithms that leverage superposition and entanglement can perform parallel computations, enabling the analysis of large datasets at unprecedented speeds. This capability allows for rapid training of models and quicker convergence, reducing the time required for machine learning tasks.

Additionally, quantum data representation opens the door to new modeling techniques that capitalize on the interconnectedness of quantum states. Quantum neural networks and quantum kernel methods can exploit entangled qubits to learn complex relationships among features, leading to more accurate predictions and improved generalization to unseen data.

The ability to represent high-dimensional data efficiently also positions quantum machine learning as a powerful tool for tackling challenges in areas such as natural language processing, image recognition, and optimization problems. As researchers explore the application of quantum data representation, the potential for breakthroughs in these domains becomes increasingly tangible.

Furthermore, the integration of quantum data representation into machine learning frameworks raises important considerations for the design and implementation of quantum algorithms. Researchers must account for the unique challenges posed by quantum measurement and decoherence when developing models and training processes.

In , the representation of quantum data is a foundational aspect of Quantum Machine Learning, shaping the development of algorithms and models that leverage the unique properties of quantum systems. As we delve deeper into the intersection of quantum computing and machine learning, the exploration of quantum data representation will serve as a crucial stepping stone toward realizing the full potential of this emerging field.

Chapter 5: Quantum Machine Learning Algorithms

Overview of Quantum Machine Learning Algorithms

Quantum Machine Learning (QML) algorithms merge the principles of quantum computing with machine learning techniques to harness the unique capabilities of quantum systems. By leveraging superposition, entanglement, and quantum parallelism, QML algorithms aim to outperform classical counterparts in tasks such as classification, clustering, regression, and optimization. The evolution of these algorithms reflects a growing understanding of how quantum mechanics can enhance data analysis and problem-solving.

The field of QML is still in its nascent stages, but several foundational algorithms have emerged that illustrate the potential benefits of quantum approaches. These algorithms often draw inspiration from classical machine learning techniques while incorporating quantum principles to improve performance. Understanding these algorithms is crucial for recognizing how quantum computing can reshape the landscape of machine learning.

The key categories of quantum machine learning algorithms include:

Quantum Supervised Learning
Quantum Unsupervised Learning
Quantum Reinforcement Learning
Quantum Kernel Methods
Quantum Neural Networks

Each category encompasses various specific algorithms, each designed to address particular challenges in machine learning while taking advantage of the unique features of quantum computing.

Quantum Supervised Learning

Quantum supervised learning focuses on using quantum algorithms to solve problems where labeled data is available. Just as classical supervised learning aims to find a mapping from inputs to outputs, quantum supervised learning algorithms leverage quantum states to learn patterns from data. Several notable algorithms have been developed in this area, demonstrating the potential advantages of quantum approaches.

Quantum Support Vector Machines

Quantum Support Vector Machines (QSVM) extend classical support vector machines to the quantum domain. In classical SVM, the goal is to find the optimal hyperplane that separates data points from different classes. QSVM utilizes quantum states to represent data points and computes the decision boundary using quantum techniques.

The main advantage of QSVM lies in its ability to handle high-dimensional feature spaces more efficiently than classical SVMs. By exploiting the quantum kernel trick, QSVM can compute the inner products of quantum states, enabling the separation of complex data distributions with fewer resources.

Quantum support vector machines have shown promise in various applications, such as image classification and text categorization. Their ability to leverage quantum parallelism allows for faster training and inference times compared to classical SVMs, particularly when working with large datasets.

Quantum Decision Trees

Quantum decision trees are an adaptation of classical decision tree algorithms, utilizing quantum gates to perform splits based on feature values. In classical decision trees, the tree structure is built recursively by selecting the best feature to split on at each node. In quantum decision trees, quantum operations can create superpositions of possible splits, allowing for more efficient exploration of the feature space.

One notable implementation of quantum decision trees is the Quantum Random Walk Decision Tree (QRWDT), which employs quantum random walks to traverse the feature space. The QRWDT can effectively capture relationships among features and make decisions based on quantum amplitudes, leading to improved classification performance.

Quantum Linear Regression

Quantum Linear Regression aims to model the relationship between input features and continuous output variables using quantum techniques. Classical linear regression minimizes the squared error between predicted and actual values, fitting a linear model to the data.

Quantum linear regression utilizes quantum circuits to perform the necessary computations. By encoding the data into quantum states, the algorithm can efficiently compute the parameters of the linear model. Techniques such as amplitude encoding allow the algorithm to leverage quantum parallelism for faster convergence.

This approach is particularly beneficial for large datasets, where classical linear regression may struggle with computational efficiency. Quantum linear regression has the potential to provide faster predictions while maintaining accuracy, making it a valuable tool for regression tasks in various applications.

Quantum Unsupervised Learning

Quantum unsupervised learning focuses on extracting patterns and structures from unlabeled data using quantum algorithms. These algorithms exploit the unique properties of quantum systems to identify relationships among data points and perform clustering, dimensionality reduction, and feature extraction.

Quantum Clustering

Quantum clustering algorithms aim to group similar data points into clusters based on their features. One of the notable quantum clustering methods is the Quantum K-Means algorithm, which extends the classical K-Means algorithm to the quantum domain.

In classical K-Means, the algorithm iteratively assigns data points to the nearest cluster centroids and updates the centroids based on the assigned points. Quantum K-Means employs quantum operations to perform these assignments and updates more efficiently. By leveraging quantum superposition, the algorithm can simultaneously explore multiple cluster assignments, potentially leading to faster convergence.

Quantum clustering algorithms have shown promise in applications such as image segmentation and anomaly detection, where identifying underlying structures in data is essential.

Quantum Principal Component Analysis

Quantum Principal Component Analysis (QPCA) is a quantum adaptation of classical PCA, a technique widely used for dimensionality reduction. Classical PCA identifies the directions of maximum variance in data and projects the data onto these principal components.

QPCA leverages quantum states to represent the data and uses quantum algorithms to compute the principal components. By exploiting quantum parallelism, QPCA can potentially provide faster computations than classical PCA, especially for high-dimensional datasets. The ability to process large datasets efficiently makes QPCA a valuable tool for data analysis and feature extraction.

Quantum Autoencoders

Quantum autoencoders are quantum neural network architectures designed for unsupervised learning tasks. These models consist of an encoder that compresses input data into a lower-dimensional representation and a decoder that reconstructs the original data from this compressed form.

Quantum autoencoders leverage quantum states to represent data points and utilize quantum gates to perform encoding and decoding operations. By incorporating quantum features, these models can learn more expressive representations of data, enhancing their performance in tasks such as denoising and anomaly detection.

Quantum Reinforcement Learning

Quantum reinforcement learning combines quantum computing with reinforcement learning techniques, enabling agents to learn from interactions with their environment using quantum algorithms. This area is still evolving, but initial research has demonstrated the potential benefits of quantum approaches in reinforcement learning scenarios.

Quantum Q-Learning

Quantum Q-learning is an adaptation of the classical Q-learning algorithm, which involves training an agent to take actions in an environment to maximize cumulative rewards. In classical Q-learning, the agent maintains a Q-table that estimates the expected return for each action in a given state.

In quantum Q-learning, the Q-values are represented as quantum states, allowing for the storage of multiple Q-values simultaneously. This encoding leverages the principles of quantum superposition to facilitate more efficient learning. By updating Q-values using quantum operations, the algorithm can potentially achieve faster convergence and improved performance in complex environments.

Quantum Policy Gradient Methods

Quantum policy gradient methods extend classical policy gradient techniques, which optimize the agent's policy directly to maximize expected rewards. These methods leverage quantum neural networks to represent policies and utilize quantum circuits for training.

By employing quantum techniques, such as variational circuits, quantum policy gradient methods can explore a larger policy space more efficiently. This exploration can lead to improved decision-making in complex environments, making quantum policy gradient methods a promising avenue for reinforcement learning.

Quantum Kernel Methods

Quantum kernel methods leverage the quantum kernel trick to compute the similarity between data points efficiently. These methods map classical data into a high-dimensional feature space using quantum operations, allowing for the use of kernel-based algorithms for classification and regression.

Quantum Support Vector Machine with Kernels

As mentioned earlier, the Quantum Support Vector Machine (QSVM) can utilize quantum kernels to compute similarities between quantum states. By applying quantum circuits to compute inner products in a high-dimensional space, QSVM can effectively separate complex data distributions.

The quantum kernel trick allows QSVM to operate in feature spaces that are challenging for classical algorithms, enabling improved classification performance on complex datasets. This approach has potential applications in various fields, including bioinformatics, finance, and image recognition.

Quantum Gaussian Processes

Quantum Gaussian Processes (QGP) extend classical Gaussian Processes to the quantum domain. Gaussian

Processes are powerful non-parametric models used for regression and classification tasks. They model the distribution of functions and provide uncertainty estimates for predictions.

In QGP, quantum techniques are employed to compute kernel matrices more efficiently. By leveraging quantum computing, QGP can potentially achieve faster training and inference times compared to classical Gaussian Processes, making them valuable for applications that require uncertainty quantification.

Quantum machine learning algorithms represent a promising frontier in the intersection of quantum computing and artificial intelligence. By harnessing the unique properties of quantum systems, these algorithms have the potential to outperform classical methods in various machine learning tasks. As research continues to advance, the development and refinement of quantum algorithms will play a critical role in unlocking the full potential of quantum machine learning.

In the subsequent chapters, we will explore the implementation of these algorithms using quantum programming frameworks, delving into practical applications and real-world case studies that highlight the transformative impact of quantum machine learning on various domains.

Chapter 6: Quantum Programming Frameworks

Introduction to Quantum Programming Frameworks

Quantum programming frameworks provide the tools and libraries necessary for developing and running quantum algorithms on quantum hardware and simulators. These frameworks are essential for researchers and developers looking to explore quantum computing's potential, as they offer high-level abstractions that simplify the complexities of quantum mechanics. By enabling users to focus on algorithm design rather than low-level implementation details, these frameworks facilitate the rapid development and experimentation of quantum algorithms, particularly in the context of quantum machine learning.

Several quantum programming frameworks have emerged in recent years, each with unique features and capabilities. Some of the most prominent frameworks include Qiskit, TensorFlow Quantum, Cirq, and PyQuil. These frameworks cater to different needs, ranging from educational purposes to advanced research applications, and they are instrumental in bridging the gap between theoretical quantum computing and practical implementation.

In this chapter, we will explore the key features of major quantum programming frameworks, their suitability for quantum machine learning tasks, and their contributions to the growing field of quantum computing.

Qiskit: An Overview

Qiskit is an open-source quantum computing framework developed by IBM. It provides a comprehensive set of tools for creating, simulating, and executing quantum algorithms on IBM's quantum processors and simulators. Qiskit's modular architecture allows users to access various components, such as quantum circuit design, simulation, and execution, making it a versatile tool for both beginners and experienced researchers.

Key Features of Qiskit

Quantum Circuit Model: Qiskit employs a circuit model for quantum computation, allowing users to build quantum circuits using a set of standard quantum gates. This model mirrors classical digital circuits, making it more accessible to those familiar with classical computing.

Modularity: The framework is organized into several modules, each focused on a specific aspect of quantum computing. The main components include:

Terra: The foundational layer that provides tools for circuit construction, transpilation, and simulation.

Aer: A high-performance simulator for testing quantum circuits and algorithms.

Ignis: A suite of tools for quantum error mitigation and characterization, essential for improving the reliability of quantum computations.

Aqua: A module specifically designed for quantum algorithms in machine learning, optimization, and chemistry.

Integration with Classical Libraries: Qiskit can be integrated with classical libraries such as NumPy and SciPy, enabling users to combine classical and quantum computations seamlessly. This integration is particularly useful in quantum machine learning applications, where hybrid algorithms may involve both classical and quantum components.

Access to Real Quantum Hardware: Qiskit allows users to execute quantum circuits on actual IBM quantum processors through the IBM Quantum Experience platform. This access is invaluable for researchers seeking to test their algorithms in real-world scenarios and gather empirical data on quantum performance.

Applications of Qiskit in Quantum Machine Learning

Qiskit provides several tools and libraries tailored for quantum machine learning tasks. For instance, the Aqua module includes a variety of quantum algorithms for supervised and unsupervised learning, quantum neural networks, and quantum kernel methods. Users can implement algorithms such as QSVM, quantum principal component analysis, and quantum clustering using the high-level abstractions provided by Qiskit.

Additionally, Qiskit's simulation capabilities allow researchers to test and refine their quantum algorithms before deploying them on actual hardware. This feature is particularly beneficial in the context of quantum machine learning, where experimentation and iteration are critical for success.

TensorFlow Quantum

TensorFlow Quantum (TFQ) is a framework developed by Google to integrate quantum machine learning into the popular TensorFlow ecosystem. TFQ combines the strengths of TensorFlow's deep learning capabilities with quantum computing, enabling users to design and train quantum models alongside classical neural networks.

Key Features of TensorFlow Quantum

Integration with TensorFlow: TFQ builds on TensorFlow's architecture, allowing users to leverage existing TensorFlow components for data preprocessing, model training, and evaluation. This integration enables the development of hybrid quantum-classical models that can exploit the strengths of both paradigms.

Quantum Circuits as Layers: TFQ treats quantum circuits as layers within a TensorFlow model. This design allows users to incorporate quantum circuits directly into neural networks, facilitating the training of quantum models using gradient-based optimization techniques.

Simulation of Quantum Circuits: TFQ provides tools for simulating quantum circuits within the TensorFlow framework, enabling users to test their models before deploying them on quantum hardware. The simulation capabilities are particularly useful for researchers exploring quantum machine learning algorithms.

Support for Quantum Data: TensorFlow Quantum includes utilities for encoding classical data into quantum states, making it easier to work with quantum representations of data in machine learning tasks.

Applications of TensorFlow Quantum in Quantum Machine Learning

TFQ is well-suited for quantum machine learning applications due to its seamless integration with classical machine learning techniques. Users can implement quantum neural networks, hybrid models, and quantum kernel methods within the TensorFlow framework, allowing for a wide range of experiments and applications.

For instance, researchers can design variational quantum circuits for classification tasks, leveraging quantum features to enhance model performance. TFQ also enables the exploration of quantum autoencoders, quantum feature maps, and other advanced quantum algorithms within the familiar TensorFlow environment.

Cirq: A Quantum Programming Framework by Google

Cirq is an open-source quantum programming framework developed by Google, designed for building and simulating quantum circuits. While Cirq is primarily focused on creating quantum algorithms for near-term quantum devices, it also offers tools for researchers interested in quantum machine learning.

Key Features of Cirq

Circuit Construction: Cirq provides a straightforward API for constructing quantum circuits using a variety of quantum gates. The framework emphasizes ease of use, allowing users to build and manipulate quantum circuits intuitively.

Noise Modeling: Cirq includes tools for modeling noise and imperfections in quantum devices, enabling researchers to simulate realistic scenarios when testing their algorithms. This feature is crucial for developing robust quantum machine learning models that can perform well in noisy environments.

Integration with Quantum Hardware: Cirq is designed to work with Google's quantum processors, allowing users to run their quantum circuits on real hardware. This capability is essential for researchers seeking to validate their quantum machine learning algorithms in practical settings.

Applications of Cirq in Quantum Machine Learning

Cirq can be utilized in various quantum machine learning tasks, particularly those involving quantum circuits and noise modeling. Researchers can implement quantum algorithms for classification, regression, and clustering using Cirq's circuit construction capabilities.

Cirq's emphasis on noise modeling makes it particularly relevant for exploring the robustness of quantum machine learning algorithms in real-world applications. By simulating noise and imperfections, researchers can develop strategies for mitigating these challenges, ensuring that their quantum models remain effective under practical conditions.

PyQuil: A Quantum Programming Framework by Rigetti

PyQuil is an open-source quantum programming framework developed by Rigetti Computing. It is designed for building and simulating quantum algorithms using Quil (Quantum Instruction Language), a low-level programming language tailored for quantum computing.

Key Features of PyQuil

Quil Language: PyQuil leverages Quil, which allows users to write quantum programs in a clear and structured manner. The Quil language is designed to be intuitive, making it accessible to those new to quantum programming.

Quantum Circuit Simulation: PyQuil provides tools for simulating quantum circuits, enabling researchers to test their algorithms before running them on real quantum hardware. The simulation capabilities are particularly valuable for exploring quantum machine learning models.

Integration with Forest Platform: PyQuil is part of Rigetti's Forest platform, which provides access to cloud-based quantum processors and simulators. This integration enables users to run their quantum programs on Rigetti's quantum hardware.

Applications of PyQuil in Quantum Machine Learning

While PyQuil is less commonly associated with quantum machine learning compared to frameworks like Qiskit and TensorFlow Quantum, it can still be utilized for developing quantum algorithms relevant to machine learning. Researchers can implement quantum clustering, quantum support vector machines, and other quantum models using PyQuil's capabilities.

PyQuil's emphasis on simulation and testing also makes it a suitable choice for exploring the robustness of quantum machine learning algorithms, allowing researchers to refine their models before deploying them on actual quantum hardware.

Comparison of Quantum Programming Frameworks

When selecting a quantum programming framework for quantum machine learning tasks, researchers must consider various factors, including ease of use, integration with classical libraries, access to quantum hardware, and specific features tailored for machine learning applications.

Ease of Use:

Qiskit and TensorFlow Quantum offer user-friendly interfaces for building and simulating quantum circuits, making them accessible to those new to quantum programming. Cirq also provides a straightforward API, while PyQuil's Quil language is designed for clarity.

Integration with Classical Libraries:

TensorFlow Quantum stands out for its seamless integration with the TensorFlow ecosystem, allowing for hybrid models that combine quantum and classical techniques. Qiskit also supports integration with classical libraries like NumPy.

Access to Quantum Hardware:

Qiskit and PyQuil provide direct access to quantum hardware through their respective platforms (IBM Quantum Experience and Rigetti's Forest). Cirq is designed for Google's quantum processors, while TensorFlow Quantum is primarily focused on simulation.

Machine Learning Features:

Qiskit's Aqua module and TensorFlow Quantum's capabilities are specifically tailored for quantum machine learning tasks, offering tools and algorithms designed for supervised and unsupervised learning. Cirq and PyQuil can also be used for quantum machine learning but may require more manual implementation.

Quantum programming frameworks are crucial for the development and implementation of quantum algorithms in machine learning and other applications. By providing the necessary tools, libraries, and access to quantum hardware, these frameworks empower

Chapter 7: Quantum Data Representation

Introduction to Quantum Data Representation

Quantum data representation is a crucial aspect of quantum machine learning, as it determines how classical data can be effectively transformed into quantum states suitable for processing by quantum algorithms. Unlike classical computing, which relies on bits that can represent either 0 or 1, quantum computing utilizes quantum bits or qubits, which can exist in superpositions of states. This inherent capability allows quantum systems to represent and process information in fundamentally different ways.

Understanding how to encode classical data into quantum states is essential for leveraging quantum computing's advantages. In this chapter, we will delve into various methods for representing data in the quantum domain, exploring both the theoretical underpinnings and practical implementations. We will examine different encoding techniques, their advantages and limitations, and the implications for quantum machine learning tasks.

Classical vs. Quantum Data Representation

In classical computing, data is represented using bits, where each bit can take on a value of either 0 or 1. This binary representation allows for straightforward manipulations and calculations using classical algorithms. However, classical data representation becomes less efficient when dealing with high-dimensional or complex datasets, which can lead to the so-called "curse of dimensionality."

In contrast, quantum data representation leverages qubits, which can exist in a superposition of states. A single qubit can represent both 0 and 1 simultaneously, leading to exponential growth in the amount of information that can be represented as more qubits are added. This property enables quantum computers to explore multiple possibilities at once, providing a significant advantage in tasks such as optimization, classification, and regression.

However, encoding classical data into quantum states requires careful consideration of how to best utilize the unique properties of quantum mechanics, including entanglement and interference. The choice of data representation can significantly impact the performance of quantum algorithms.

Data Encoding Techniques

Several data encoding techniques have been developed to transform classical data into quantum states. Each technique has its strengths and weaknesses, and the choice of encoding method can depend on the specific quantum algorithm being used and the nature of the data being processed. Below are some of the most commonly used data encoding techniques in quantum machine learning:

Amplitude Encoding

Amplitude encoding is a widely used technique for representing classical data in quantum states. In this method, classical data points are mapped to the amplitudes of a quantum state. Specifically, if a dataset contains nnn classical data points, these points can be encoded into a mmm-qubit quantum state, where m=⌈log⬜2(n)⌉m = \lceil \log_2(n) \rceil m=⌈log2(n)⌉.

For example, consider a classical vector x=[x1,x2,…,xn]\mathbf{x} = [x_1, x_2, \ldots, x_n]x=[x1,x2,…,xn]. Amplitude encoding constructs a quantum state |ψ⟩|\psi\rangle|ψ⟩ such that:

|ψ⟩=1N∑i=1Nxi|i⟩|\psi\rangle = \frac{1}{\sqrt{N}} \sum_{i=1}^{N} x_i |i\rangle|ψ⟩=N1i=1∑Nxi|i⟩

where |i⟩|i\rangle|i⟩ represents the computational basis states of the qubits. This representation allows the quantum state to encode the entire vector in a compact form, exploiting the superposition of states.

The advantage of amplitude encoding is its ability to efficiently represent high-dimensional data in a low-dimensional quantum state. However, a notable limitation is that the classical data must be normalized to ensure that the sum of the squares of the amplitudes equals one.

Basis Encoding

Basis encoding is another straightforward technique where classical data is directly mapped to the computational basis states of qubits. In this approach, each classical data point is represented as a unique computational basis state. For example, if there are NNN classical data points, they can be represented using mmm qubits, where m=⌈log⌐2(N)⌉m = \lceil \log_2(N) \rceilm=⌈log2(N)⌉.

For a classical dataset {d1,d2,…,dN}\{d_1, d_2, \ldots, d_N\}{d1,d2,…,dN}, the corresponding quantum states would be:

|di⟩for i=1,2,…,N|d_i\rangle \quad \text{for } i = 1, 2, \ldots, N|di⟩for i=1,2,…,N

This method is simple and intuitive but can lead to inefficiencies, especially with large datasets. The main drawback is that as the number of data points increases, the number of qubits required grows logarithmically, which may not always be practical for quantum algorithms.

Angle Encoding

Angle encoding is a technique that maps classical data points to the angles of quantum rotations. In this method, each classical data point is represented by a rotation of a qubit around the Bloch sphere. For instance, if a classical data point xxx is mapped to a qubit, the corresponding quantum state can be represented as:

$|\psi\rangle=\cos(x2)|0\rangle+\sin(x2)|1\rangle$ $\psi\rangle = \cos\left(\frac{x}{2}\right)|0\rangle + \sin\left(\frac{x}{2}\right)|1\rangle|\psi\rangle=\cos(2x)|0\rangle+\sin(2x)|1\rangle$

This representation allows for a smooth transition between classical and quantum states and can effectively utilize continuous data. The main advantage of angle encoding is that it provides a natural way to represent real-valued data in quantum circuits.

However, angle encoding may require more qubits than amplitude encoding when dealing with large datasets, as the number of qubits needed increases with the dimensionality of the input data. Moreover, the encoding process may introduce additional complexity when integrating with quantum algorithms.

Quantum Feature Maps

Quantum feature maps are techniques that encode classical data into a higher-dimensional quantum state using quantum gates. This method is often utilized in quantum kernel methods, where the goal is to map classical data into a quantum feature space that enables better separation of data points for classification tasks.

For example, a classical data point xxx can be transformed using a sequence of quantum gates to create a quantum state $|\phi(x)\rangle$ |\phi(x)\rangle|$\phi(x)\rangle$ in a higher-dimensional Hilbert space. The advantage of this technique is that it allows for the exploration of complex relationships between data points, potentially leading to improved performance in machine learning tasks.

Quantum feature maps can be constructed using various techniques, such as variational circuits, which combine classical optimization with quantum circuits. These feature maps enhance the expressiveness of quantum models, making them suitable for complex datasets.

Considerations for Quantum Data Representation

When selecting a data representation technique for quantum machine learning tasks, several factors must be considered:

Dimensionality:

The dimensionality of the classical data can significantly influence the choice of encoding method. For high-dimensional data, amplitude encoding may be more efficient, while for lower-dimensional datasets, basis encoding may suffice.

Data Type:

The nature of the data (e.g., categorical, continuous) can also dictate the appropriate encoding method. Angle encoding is particularly useful for continuous data, while basis encoding is more suited for discrete data points.

Algorithm Requirements:

Different quantum algorithms may necessitate specific data representations. For instance, quantum kernel methods may require quantum feature maps, while quantum neural networks may benefit from angle or amplitude encoding.

Noise Resilience:

In near-term quantum devices, noise and errors can significantly affect computations. Data representation techniques that mitigate these issues are essential for developing robust quantum machine learning models.

Practical Implementations of Quantum Data Representation

Implementing quantum data representation techniques requires familiarity with quantum programming frameworks such as Qiskit, TensorFlow Quantum, or Cirq. These frameworks provide the necessary tools for encoding classical data into quantum states and integrating them into quantum algorithms.

Example: Amplitude Encoding in Qiskit

To demonstrate amplitude encoding in Qiskit, one might start by defining a classical dataset and normalizing it. The following Python code snippet illustrates how to encode a classical vector into a quantum state using Qiskit:

```python
Copy code
from qiskit import QuantumCircuit, Aer, transpile,
assemble, execute
import numpy as np

# Classical data
data = np.array([0.1, 0.2, 0.3, 0.4])
```

```
normalized_data = data / np.linalg.norm(data)

# Create a quantum circuit
num_qubits = int(np.ceil(np.log2(len(normalized_data))))
qc = QuantumCircuit(num_qubits)

# Amplitude encoding
for i, amplitude in enumerate(normalized_data):
qc.initialize(np.sqrt(amplitude)   *   np.array([1,   0])   +
np.sqrt(1 - amplitude) * np.array([0, 1]), i)

# Simulate the circuit
backend = Aer.get_backend('statevector_simulator')
qc = transpile(qc, backend)
qobj = assemble(qc)
result = execute(qc, backend).result()
statevector = result.get_statevector()

print("Encoded state:", statevector)
```

In this example, we define a classical dataset, normalize it, and create a quantum circuit that encodes the data using amplitude encoding. The resulting quantum state can then be used in various quantum algorithms.

Example: Angle Encoding in TensorFlow Quantum

In TensorFlow Quantum, angle encoding can be implemented by using quantum layers that rotate qubits based on classical data. Below is a simple illustration of how to use angle encoding in a quantum model:

python
Copy code

```python
import tensorflow as tf
import tensorflow_quantum as tfq
import cirq

# Define a quantum circuit for angle encoding
def create_circuit(data):
circuit = cirq.Circuit()
circuit.append(cirq.rx(data[0])(cirq.GridQubit(0,   0)))      # Rotate based on data
return circuit

# Example data
classical_data = np.array([0.5, 0.8])

# Create the quantum circuit
quantum_circuit = create_circuit(classical_data)

# Integrate into a quantum model (e.g., using quantum layers)
# This part would involve defining a full quantum neural network model
```

Chapter 8: Quantum Machine Learning Algorithms

Introduction to Quantum Machine Learning Algorithms

Quantum machine learning (QML) algorithms leverage the principles of quantum computing to process and analyze data in ways that can surpass classical methods. By utilizing quantum states, entanglement, and superposition, QML algorithms can potentially achieve significant speedups in training and inference compared to their classical counterparts. This chapter will explore several foundational quantum machine learning algorithms, their theoretical underpinnings, and practical implementations using frameworks like Qiskit and TensorFlow Quantum.

Quantum machine learning algorithms can be categorized into several types, including supervised learning, unsupervised learning, and reinforcement learning. Each category has distinct algorithms that can exploit the advantages of quantum computation. By examining these algorithms, we can gain insights into their capabilities, applications, and limitations in various domains.

Supervised Learning Algorithms

Supervised learning is a type of machine learning where the model is trained on labeled data, allowing it to learn the mapping between inputs and outputs. Several quantum algorithms have been developed for supervised learning tasks, including classification and regression.

Quantum Support Vector Machines (QSVM)

Quantum Support Vector Machines (QSVM) extend the classical support vector machine framework into the quantum domain. The core idea behind SVMs is to find a hyperplane that best separates different classes of data points in a high-dimensional feature space. QSVM leverages quantum computing's ability to efficiently process high-dimensional data, potentially improving classification performance.

The QSVM algorithm can be described as follows:

Data Encoding: Classical data is encoded into quantum states using techniques such as amplitude or basis encoding.

Feature Mapping: The quantum feature map transforms the classical data into a higher-dimensional Hilbert space, enabling better separation of classes.

Optimization: A quantum algorithm, such as the Quantum Approximate Optimization Algorithm (QAOA), is used to find the optimal hyperplane that separates the classes.

Measurement: The quantum state is measured to obtain the final classification result.

QSVM shows promise in scenarios where classical SVMs struggle, particularly in high-dimensional datasets. However, its practical application is still being explored, and scalability remains a challenge.

Variational Quantum Classifiers (VQC)

Variational Quantum Classifiers (VQC) are quantum circuits parameterized by classical parameters that are optimized to minimize a cost function, typically related to the classification error. VQC combines the power of quantum circuits with classical optimization techniques.

The process involves:

Circuit Construction: A quantum circuit is created with parameters that will be optimized. The circuit typically consists of layers of quantum gates applied to qubits.
Data Encoding: Classical data is encoded into the quantum state of the circuit, often using angle encoding or amplitude encoding.
Cost Function Evaluation: The circuit is run on a quantum simulator or hardware, and a cost function is evaluated based on the measurement outcomes.
Optimization: Classical optimization algorithms, such as gradient descent or genetic algorithms, are used to update the circuit parameters iteratively.
Prediction: After training, the optimized circuit can be used to make predictions on new data.

VQCs have gained attention due to their flexibility and ability to incorporate classical and quantum elements, making them suitable for a wide range of classification tasks.

Quantum Neural Networks (QNN)

Quantum Neural Networks (QNN) attempt to adapt classical neural network structures to the quantum realm. QNNs can capture complex relationships in data by leveraging quantum features and parallelism.

The architecture of a QNN typically includes:

Quantum Layers: Each layer of the network consists of quantum gates that operate on qubits, creating quantum states representative of the input data.

Activation Functions: QNNs employ quantum analogs of classical activation functions, which help determine the output of each neuron.

Training: Similar to classical neural networks, QNNs are trained using backpropagation and optimization techniques, adjusting the parameters of quantum gates to minimize the error.

Inference: Once trained, the QNN can be used for tasks such as classification and regression by processing new input data through the quantum layers.

QNNs offer the potential for enhanced expressiveness and performance, especially for problems with complex relationships in the data. However, practical implementations and scaling remain ongoing challenges.

Unsupervised Learning Algorithms

Unsupervised learning involves training models on unlabeled data, aiming to discover patterns or structures within the data. Quantum algorithms for unsupervised learning can efficiently perform clustering, dimensionality reduction, and data generation.

Quantum k-Means Clustering

Quantum k-means clustering adapts the classical k-means algorithm to the quantum domain. The k-means algorithm partitions data points into kkk clusters based on their distances to cluster centroids.

The quantum k-means algorithm operates as follows:

Data Encoding: Classical data points are encoded into quantum states.

Distance Calculation: Quantum circuits are used to compute the distances between data points and cluster centroids. This can be done using quantum features to leverage the advantages of superposition and entanglement.

Centroid Update: The algorithm iteratively updates the cluster centroids based on the assigned data points until convergence.

Measurement: Final cluster assignments are obtained through quantum measurements.

Quantum k-means can offer speedups over classical implementations, particularly for large datasets. However, the complexity of the quantum distance calculations and convergence guarantees remain areas of research.

Quantum Principal Component Analysis (QPCA)

Quantum Principal Component Analysis (QPCA) aims to extract the most significant features of high-dimensional data by identifying the principal components that capture the variance. QPCA utilizes quantum algorithms to efficiently compute the eigenvalues and eigenvectors of the covariance matrix.

The QPCA process involves:

Data Encoding: Classical data is encoded into quantum states.

Covariance Matrix Construction: A quantum circuit is constructed to prepare and manipulate the covariance matrix of the data.

Eigenvalue Decomposition: Quantum algorithms, such as the Harrow-Hassidim-Lloyd (HHL) algorithm, are employed to compute the eigenvalues and eigenvectors of the covariance matrix.

Feature Extraction: The principal components are extracted, providing a reduced representation of the original data.

QPCA can provide significant speedups over classical PCA, especially in high-dimensional datasets. However, challenges related to noise and hardware limitations remain critical considerations.

Reinforcement Learning Algorithms

Reinforcement learning (RL) involves training agents to make sequential decisions based on feedback from their environment. Quantum algorithms for reinforcement learning aim to enhance the exploration and exploitation capabilities of classical RL methods.

Quantum Reinforcement Learning (QRL)

Quantum Reinforcement Learning (QRL) combines the principles of quantum computing with classical reinforcement learning techniques. QRL algorithms can utilize quantum states to represent the agent's policy and value functions, potentially enabling more efficient exploration of state spaces.

Key components of QRL include:

Quantum Policy Representation: The policy of the agent is represented as a quantum state, allowing for superposition over multiple actions.

Quantum Value Function: The value function, which estimates the expected returns from a state, can also be represented using quantum states.

Quantum Exploration Strategies: QRL algorithms may incorporate quantum strategies for exploration, such as using quantum amplitude amplification to favor promising actions or states.

Learning and Updates: The learning process involves updating the quantum states representing the policy and value function based on feedback from the environment.

QRL is still an emerging field, and practical implementations are under exploration. However, the potential for enhanced exploration and improved convergence rates makes QRL a promising area of research.

Practical Implementations of Quantum Machine Learning Algorithms

Implementing quantum machine learning algorithms involves utilizing quantum programming frameworks that provide the necessary tools for constructing and executing quantum circuits. Below are examples of how to implement two prominent QML algorithms: QSVM and VQC using Qiskit.

Example: Quantum Support Vector Machine in Qiskit

The following code snippet illustrates a simple implementation of QSVM in Qiskit:

```python
Copy code
from qiskit import QuantumCircuit, Aer
from qiskit.aer import AerSimulator
from qiskit.utils import QuantumInstance
from qiskit_machine_learning.algorithms import QSVC

# Sample dataset
X_train = [[0, 0], [0, 1], [1, 0], [1, 1]]
y_train = [0, 1, 1, 0]

# Create a QSVM instance
qsvc                                    =
QSVC(quantum_instance=QuantumInstance(Aer.get_back
end('aer_simulator')))

# Fit the model
```

```python
qsvc.fit(X_train, y_train)

# Predictions
predictions = qsvc.predict([[0, 0], [1, 1]])
print("Predictions:", predictions)
```

In this example, we define a simple training dataset, create a QSVM instance, fit the model, and make predictions. This highlights how Qiskit facilitates the implementation of quantum algorithms.

Example: Variational Quantum Classifier in TensorFlow Quantum

The following code snippet illustrates a basic implementation of a VQC in TensorFlow Quantum:

```python
python
Copy code
import tensorflow as tf
import tensorflow_quantum as tfq
import cirq

# Define a simple quantum circuit
def create_circuit(data):
circuit = cirq.Circuit()
circuit.append(cirq.rx(data[0])(cirq.GridQubit(0,  0)))    # Encode data
circuit.append(cirq.ry(data[1])(cirq.GridQubit(0, 1)))
return circuit
```

```
# Build the model
model = tf.keras.Sequential([
tfq.layers.PQC(create_circuit, cirq.Z(cirq.GridQ
```

Chapter 9: Quantum Algorithms for Optimization

Introduction to Quantum Optimization Algorithms

Optimization problems are central to many fields, including machine learning, finance, logistics, and engineering. Classical algorithms often struggle with large or complex optimization problems due to their computational intensity. Quantum optimization algorithms leverage the principles of quantum mechanics, such as superposition and entanglement, to explore solution spaces more efficiently than classical counterparts. This chapter will delve into various quantum algorithms designed for optimization tasks, highlighting their theoretical foundations, applications, and practical implementations.

Quantum optimization can be categorized into two primary approaches: variational methods and combinatorial optimization algorithms. Each approach has distinct characteristics and applications, making them suitable for different types of optimization problems.

Variational Optimization Algorithms

Variational optimization methods involve parameterized quantum circuits that can be optimized to find the best solutions to specific problems. These methods often rely on classical optimization techniques to adjust the parameters of the quantum circuits.

Quantum Approximate Optimization Algorithm (QAOA)

The Quantum Approximate Optimization Algorithm (QAOA) is a prominent variational approach designed to solve combinatorial optimization problems. QAOA aims to find the optimal solution by maximizing an objective function defined over a set of feasible solutions.

The QAOA process involves the following steps:

Problem Encoding: The optimization problem is encoded into a cost function that can be evaluated on a quantum circuit.

Quantum Circuit Construction: A parameterized quantum circuit is constructed with layers of quantum gates, including problem-specific unitaries and mixing unitaries.

Parameter Optimization: Classical optimization techniques are used to adjust the parameters of the quantum circuit to minimize the cost function.

Measurement: The quantum state is measured to extract the solution, which is then evaluated against the objective function.

QAOA has shown promise for various optimization problems, including Max-Cut and other combinatorial tasks. However, its effectiveness may be influenced by factors such as circuit depth and noise.

Variational Quantum Eigensolver (VQE)

The Variational Quantum Eigensolver (VQE) is primarily used for solving quantum chemistry problems, specifically for finding the ground state energy of quantum systems. VQE combines quantum circuits with classical optimization to explore the energy landscape of quantum systems.

The VQE process consists of:

Hamiltonian Encoding: The Hamiltonian of the quantum system is expressed as a linear combination of Pauli operators.
Parameterization: A parameterized quantum circuit is designed to prepare quantum states that approximate the ground state of the system.
Energy Evaluation: The expectation value of the Hamiltonian is computed using quantum measurements.
Optimization: Classical optimization algorithms are employed to minimize the energy expectation value by adjusting the circuit parameters.

VQE has been successful in various applications, particularly in simulating molecular systems, and serves as a foundational algorithm in quantum chemistry.

Combinatorial Optimization Algorithms

Combinatorial optimization involves finding the best solution from a finite set of possibilities, often under specific constraints. Quantum algorithms for combinatorial optimization can exploit quantum properties to enhance solution exploration.

Quantum Adiabatic Optimization (QAO)

Quantum Adiabatic Optimization (QAO) is based on the adiabatic theorem of quantum mechanics, which states that a system can be transitioned from an initial Hamiltonian to a final Hamiltonian without exciting the system, provided the transition is slow enough.

The QAO process includes:

Initial Hamiltonian: The initial Hamiltonian is chosen to have an easily identifiable ground state.
Final Hamiltonian: The final Hamiltonian encodes the objective function of the optimization problem.
Adiabatic Evolution: The system is gradually evolved from the initial Hamiltonian to the final Hamiltonian, ideally remaining in the ground state throughout the process.
Measurement: The final state is measured to extract the optimal solution.

QAO has the potential to solve complex combinatorial problems, but its practical implementation is limited by the need for slow adiabatic evolution and the challenges posed by noise.

Grover's Search Algorithm

Grover's Search Algorithm is a quantum algorithm designed for searching unsorted databases. It can be applied to optimization problems by identifying solutions that satisfy certain criteria more efficiently than classical brute-force methods.

The steps involved in Grover's algorithm are:

Oracle Construction: An oracle is constructed to mark the solutions that meet the desired criteria.

Superposition: The algorithm prepares a superposition of all possible solutions.

Grover Iterations: The algorithm iteratively amplifies the probability amplitudes of the marked solutions through a series of operations, including inversion about the mean.

Measurement: After a predetermined number of iterations, the state is measured, yielding a solution with a high probability.

Grover's algorithm offers a quadratic speedup for unstructured search problems, making it valuable for certain optimization tasks.

Practical Implementations of Quantum Optimization Algorithms

Implementing quantum optimization algorithms requires leveraging quantum programming frameworks to construct and execute quantum circuits. Below are examples of how to implement QAOA and VQE using Qiskit.

Example: Quantum Approximate Optimization Algorithm in Qiskit

The following code snippet illustrates a simple implementation of QAOA in Qiskit:

python
Copy code

```python
from qiskit import Aer
from qiskit.circuit import QuantumCircuit
from qiskit.algorithms import NumPyMinimumEigensolver
from qiskit.algorithms.optimizers import SLSQP
from qiskit.utils import QuantumInstance
from qiskit.algorithms import QAOA

# Define the problem (e.g., Max-Cut)
w = [[0, 1], [1, 0]]  # Adjacency matrix for a simple graph
num_nodes = len(w)

# Create a QAOA instance
optimizer = SLSQP(maxiter=100)
qaoa = QAOA(optimizer=optimizer)

# Run QAOA
result = qaoa.compute_minimum_eigenvalue(operator=w)

print("Optimal value:", result.eigenvalue)
```

In this example, we define a simple Max-Cut problem, create a QAOA instance, and run it to find the optimal value.

Example: Variational Quantum Eigensolver in Qiskit

The following code snippet illustrates a basic implementation of VQE in Qiskit:

```python
Copy code
from qiskit import Aer
from qiskit.algorithms import VQE
from qiskit.circuit.library import TwoLocal
from qiskit.utils import QuantumInstance
from qiskit.quantum_info import Pauli

# Define the Hamiltonian (example: H2 molecule)
hamiltonian = Pauli('ZZ')  # Simple example; usually derived from a molecular Hamiltonian

# Create a VQE instance
vqe = VQE(ansatz=TwoLocal(rotation_blocks='ry', entanglement='full'), optimizer=SLSQP())

# Run VQE
result = vqe.compute_minimum_eigenvalue(operator=hamiltonian)

print("Ground state energy:", result.eigenvalue)
```

In this example, we define a simple Hamiltonian, create a VQE instance, and run it to find the ground state energy.

Quantum optimization algorithms represent a promising frontier in computational methods, potentially offering significant speedups for complex problems. While many algorithms are still in their infancy, ongoing research and development in quantum hardware and software are likely to enhance their practical applicability. Understanding these algorithms' theoretical foundations and practical implementations can pave the way for advancements in various domains, from machine learning to materials science.

Chapter 10: Quantum Data Processing Techniques

Introduction to Quantum Data Processing Techniques

Quantum data processing techniques are essential for harnessing the power of quantum computing to manipulate, analyze, and derive insights from quantum-encoded data. Unlike classical data processing, which relies on linear algebra and classical algorithms, quantum data processing leverages quantum mechanics principles, such as superposition and entanglement, to perform complex computations more efficiently. This chapter explores various quantum data processing techniques, their theoretical foundations, practical implementations, and their implications for fields like quantum machine learning and data science.

Quantum Data Processing Frameworks

Several frameworks facilitate quantum data processing, enabling researchers and practitioners to implement quantum algorithms efficiently. Two prominent frameworks are Qiskit and TensorFlow Quantum, which provide tools for constructing quantum circuits, performing data processing tasks, and integrating quantum algorithms into machine learning workflows.

Qiskit

Qiskit is an open-source quantum computing framework developed by IBM. It offers a comprehensive suite of tools for quantum circuit construction, simulation, and execution on real quantum devices. Qiskit allows users to create quantum circuits using Python, enabling easy manipulation of quantum states and measurement.

Key features of Qiskit include:

Circuit Composer: A graphical interface for building quantum circuits.
Quantum Simulators: Tools for simulating quantum circuits on classical hardware.
Hardware Access: Capability to run circuits on IBM's quantum devices via the cloud.
Quantum Machine Learning: Integration with classical machine learning libraries, allowing for hybrid models.

Qiskit's modular architecture enables users to customize and extend its functionalities, making it a popular choice for researchers and developers in quantum computing.

TensorFlow Quantum

TensorFlow Quantum (TFQ) is a library built on top of TensorFlow, designed specifically for quantum machine learning applications. TFQ combines quantum circuits with classical machine learning workflows, enabling seamless integration of quantum data processing with classical training and inference techniques.

Key features of TFQ include:

Quantum Layers: Layers that combine quantum circuits with classical neural networks.

Cirq Integration: Integration with Cirq, a quantum computing library, to build quantum circuits.

Hybrid Models: Support for models that combine classical and quantum components.

Data Processing Pipelines: Tools for preprocessing quantum data and training quantum models.

TFQ empowers machine learning practitioners to explore quantum algorithms without requiring extensive knowledge of quantum mechanics.

Quantum State Preparation

Preparing quantum states is a fundamental aspect of quantum data processing. The effectiveness of quantum algorithms often hinges on the quality of the quantum states used as inputs. Various techniques exist for preparing quantum states from classical data, each with its strengths and limitations.

Amplitude Encoding

As discussed in earlier chapters, amplitude encoding is a technique where classical data is represented as the amplitudes of a quantum state. This approach allows for efficient encoding of high-dimensional data into a compact quantum state. The key advantage of amplitude encoding is its ability to represent N classical data points using only $O(\log N)$ qubits.

To prepare a quantum state using amplitude encoding, the classical data must be normalized to ensure that the sum of the squared amplitudes equals one. The quantum state is then constructed using quantum gates to create superpositions of the encoded amplitudes.

Basis Encoding

Basis encoding directly maps classical data points to the computational basis states of qubits. This technique is straightforward but can be inefficient for large datasets, as the number of qubits required grows logarithmically with the number of data points. Basis encoding is often used for discrete data and can serve as a starting point for more complex data preparation techniques.

Angle Encoding

Angle encoding involves representing classical data points as rotations on the Bloch sphere. Each classical data point is associated with a quantum state that corresponds to a rotation of a qubit around a specific axis. This technique is particularly effective for continuous data, as it allows for smooth transitions between states and can capture a range of values.

The advantage of angle encoding lies in its ability to represent real-valued data efficiently, though it may require more qubits compared to other encoding methods for high-dimensional datasets.

Quantum Feature Maps

Quantum feature maps enable the encoding of classical data into higher-dimensional quantum states. This technique is commonly used in quantum kernel methods, where the goal is to create a quantum representation that enhances the separation of data points for classification tasks.

Quantum feature maps can be constructed using a series of quantum gates applied to qubits, allowing the model to exploit the rich structure of quantum states for complex datasets. The choice of feature map can significantly influence the performance of quantum algorithms in machine learning tasks.

Quantum Circuit Design

Designing quantum circuits is a crucial aspect of quantum data processing. Quantum circuits consist of a sequence of quantum gates applied to qubits, and the design process involves determining the optimal configuration of gates to achieve the desired quantum operations.

Quantum Gates

Quantum gates are the building blocks of quantum circuits, analogous to classical logic gates. They manipulate qubits and create quantum states through unitary transformations. Common types of quantum gates include:

Single-Qubit Gates: Gates that operate on a single qubit, such as the Pauli gates (X, Y, Z), Hadamard (H), and rotation gates (Rx, Ry, Rz).
Multi-Qubit Gates: Gates that operate on multiple qubits, such as the CNOT (controlled-NOT) gate, which entangles qubits.

When designing quantum circuits, it is essential to consider the specific operations required for data processing tasks, as well as the coherence time and noise characteristics of the quantum hardware being used.

Circuit Depth and Complexity

The depth of a quantum circuit refers to the number of sequential operations applied to the qubits. Circuit depth is a critical factor in determining the performance and feasibility of quantum algorithms, as deeper circuits are more susceptible to noise and errors.

When designing quantum circuits, it is important to balance circuit depth and complexity to ensure that the quantum operations can be executed accurately. Techniques such as circuit optimization and gate synthesis can help reduce circuit depth while maintaining functionality.

Error Mitigation Techniques

Quantum circuits are subject to errors due to noise in quantum hardware. Error mitigation techniques aim to reduce the impact of these errors on the final results. Common strategies include:

Dynamical Decoupling: A technique that applies a sequence of control pulses to decouple qubits from their environment, reducing decoherence.

Error Correction Codes: Quantum error correction codes, such as surface codes, protect quantum information by encoding it across multiple qubits.

Post-Processing: Techniques that adjust the results of quantum measurements to account for known errors, improving the accuracy of final outputs.

Implementing these error mitigation strategies can enhance the reliability of quantum data processing and improve the quality of results obtained from quantum algorithms.

Quantum Measurement Techniques

Measurement is a crucial step in quantum data processing, as it determines the outcome of quantum computations. Unlike classical measurements, which provide definite results, quantum measurements yield probabilistic outcomes based on the quantum state.

Measurement Operators

In quantum mechanics, measurements are performed using measurement operators, which project quantum states onto classical outcomes. The choice of measurement operator can significantly influence the results obtained from a quantum algorithm.

Common measurement operators include:

Projective Measurements: Measurements that project a quantum state onto a specific basis, collapsing it into one of the basis states.
Observables: Operators that correspond to measurable quantities in quantum systems, allowing for the extraction of meaningful information from quantum states.

The design of measurement operators should align with the goals of the quantum data processing task, ensuring that relevant information is captured.

Classical Post-Processing

After performing quantum measurements, classical post-processing is often required to analyze the results and extract insights. Classical algorithms can be applied to the measurement outcomes to perform tasks such as:

Statistical Analysis: Evaluating the distribution of measurement outcomes to derive probabilities and statistics.
Data Interpretation: Interpreting the results in the context of the original problem, allowing for meaningful s to be drawn.

Effective classical post-processing techniques are essential for translating quantum measurement outcomes into actionable insights.

Applications of Quantum Data Processing Techniques

Quantum data processing techniques have the potential to revolutionize various fields by enabling more efficient data analysis, enhanced pattern recognition, and improved decision-making. Several application areas where quantum data processing can make a significant impact include:

Quantum Machine Learning

Quantum data processing techniques play a vital role in quantum machine learning applications. By efficiently encoding and processing data, quantum algorithms can enhance classification, clustering, and regression tasks, enabling models that can outperform classical counterparts in specific scenarios.

Quantum Chemistry and Material Science

Quantum data processing is essential in simulating quantum systems, such as molecules and materials. Techniques like VQE enable researchers to study molecular properties, predict chemical reactions, and explore novel materials with enhanced functionalities.

Financial Modeling

Quantum data processing techniques can be applied to optimize financial portfolios, assess risk, and model complex financial systems. By leveraging quantum algorithms, financial analysts can uncover insights that may be challenging to obtain through classical methods.

Optimization Problems

Quantum data processing techniques are well-suited for solving optimization problems in logistics, supply chain management, and scheduling. By efficiently exploring solution spaces, quantum algorithms can identify optimal solutions more rapidly than classical approaches.

Practical Implementations of Quantum Data Processing Techniques

Implementing quantum data processing techniques involves using frameworks like Qiskit and TensorFlow Quantum to prepare quantum states, design quantum circuits, and perform measurements. Below are examples of implementing quantum state preparation and measurement using Qiskit.

Example: Quantum State Preparation with Amplitude Encoding in Qiskit

python
Copy code

```python
from qiskit import QuantumCircuit, Aer, transpile,
assemble, execute
import numpy as np

# Classical data
data = np.array([
```

Chapter 11: Quantum Hardware and Quantum Computing Platforms

Introduction to Quantum Hardware and Platforms

Quantum hardware serves as the physical backbone for executing quantum algorithms and processing quantum data. Unlike classical computers, which utilize bits as the fundamental unit of information, quantum computers leverage quantum bits or qubits, which can exist in multiple states simultaneously due to the principles of superposition and entanglement. This chapter explores the different types of quantum hardware, the various quantum computing platforms available, and the implications for quantum machine learning and other applications.

Understanding the architecture of quantum hardware is essential for anyone looking to delve into quantum computing. The choices made in hardware design influence the performance, scalability, and error rates of quantum computations.

Types of Quantum Hardware

Quantum hardware can be classified into several categories based on the underlying technology used to implement qubits. Each type has its unique advantages and challenges, impacting the efficiency and applicability of quantum algorithms.

Superconducting Qubits

Superconducting qubits are one of the most widely used types of qubits in current quantum computing research. These qubits are based on superconducting circuits that can exhibit quantum behavior at very low temperatures.

Key features of superconducting qubits include:

Fast Gate Operations: Superconducting qubits allow for rapid gate operations, often on the order of nanoseconds.
Scalability: Researchers have developed techniques for scaling up superconducting qubit systems, making them suitable for larger quantum processors.
Integration with Classical Electronics: Superconducting qubits can be integrated with classical electronics, facilitating easier control and measurement.

However, superconducting qubits are also susceptible to decoherence and noise, requiring error correction techniques to maintain fidelity in computations.

Trapped Ion Qubits

Trapped ion qubits utilize ions confined in electromagnetic fields to create qubits. These ions can be manipulated using lasers, which induce quantum gates through precise control of their internal states.

Key features of trapped ion qubits include:

Long Coherence Times: Trapped ion qubits exhibit longer coherence times compared to many other qubit types, making them suitable for high-fidelity quantum operations.

High Precision: Laser-based control allows for precise manipulation of quantum states, enabling effective implementation of quantum algorithms.

Entanglement: Trapped ions can be easily entangled, a crucial feature for quantum algorithms that require entanglement.

Despite these advantages, trapped ion systems face challenges related to scalability and speed, as operations can be slower than superconducting qubits.

Quantum Dots

Quantum dots are semiconductor nanostructures that can confine electrons and exhibit quantum behavior. By manipulating the charge and spin states of electrons in these dots, researchers can implement qubits.

Key features of quantum dots include:

Integration with Classical Technology: Quantum dots can be integrated into existing semiconductor technology, making them attractive for future quantum computing architectures.

Potential for Scalability: The use of standard semiconductor fabrication techniques offers pathways for scalable quantum processors.

Versatility: Quantum dots can potentially be used for both quantum computing and quantum communication applications.

However, achieving precise control over the quantum states in quantum dots remains a significant challenge.

Topological Qubits

Topological qubits are a theoretical approach that utilizes anyons—exotic particles that exist in two-dimensional systems—to encode quantum information. These qubits are believed to be more resistant to decoherence due to their topological nature.

Key features of topological qubits include:

Robustness to Errors: Topological qubits are theorized to be more robust against local perturbations, making them attractive for fault-tolerant quantum computing.

Error Correction: The nature of topological states could simplify error correction methods, allowing for more efficient quantum computations.

While topological qubits are still largely in the research phase, they hold promise for future quantum computing systems due to their potential resilience against noise.

Quantum Computing Platforms

Numerous quantum computing platforms are available today, each with unique features and capabilities. These platforms allow researchers to develop, test, and run quantum algorithms on real quantum hardware.

IBM Quantum Experience

IBM Quantum Experience is a cloud-based quantum computing platform that provides access to IBM's superconducting qubit devices. It features a user-friendly interface that allows users to create and run quantum circuits on actual quantum processors.

Key features of IBM Quantum Experience include:

Real-Time Access: Users can run experiments on real quantum hardware, providing hands-on experience with quantum algorithms.

Qiskit Integration: The platform seamlessly integrates with Qiskit, allowing users to construct quantum circuits and algorithms using Python.

Educational Resources: IBM provides a wealth of tutorials and resources to help users learn quantum computing concepts and programming.

IBM Quantum Experience is suitable for both beginners and experienced researchers, making it a popular choice for quantum computing education and research.

Google Quantum AI

Google Quantum AI focuses on developing quantum processors based on superconducting qubit technology. The platform aims to achieve quantum supremacy by demonstrating that quantum computers can solve problems beyond the capabilities of classical computers.

Key features of Google Quantum AI include:

Sycamore Processor: The Sycamore quantum processor is designed for high-performance quantum computations, featuring a complex architecture to facilitate entanglement.

Quantum Algorithms Research: Google actively conducts research on quantum algorithms, aiming to push the boundaries of what is possible with quantum computing.

Collaboration and Open Source: Google promotes collaboration with the quantum research community and has open-sourced its quantum programming framework, Cirq.

Google Quantum AI is at the forefront of quantum research and is instrumental in advancing the field.

Rigetti Quantum Cloud Services

Rigetti offers a cloud-based quantum computing platform called Rigetti Quantum Cloud Services, which provides access to its superconducting qubit devices. The platform focuses on making quantum computing accessible to developers and researchers.

Key features of Rigetti Quantum Cloud Services include:

Forest SDK: Rigetti's Forest SDK allows users to develop quantum programs and run them on real quantum hardware.
Hybrid Computing Models: The platform supports hybrid computing models, integrating quantum and classical algorithms for enhanced performance.
User-Friendly Interface: Rigetti provides a user-friendly interface for creating and executing quantum circuits, making it accessible to a broader audience.

Rigetti's focus on user accessibility and hybrid models makes it an attractive platform for quantum computing research.

Microsoft Quantum Development Kit

Microsoft's Quantum Development Kit (QDK) is a comprehensive framework for quantum programming, including the Q# programming language specifically designed for quantum algorithms. The QDK provides tools for developing, testing, and simulating quantum applications.

Key features of Microsoft QDK include:

Q# Language: Q# is a domain-specific language designed for quantum programming, allowing users to express quantum algorithms concisely.

Integration with Visual Studio: The QDK integrates with Visual Studio, providing a familiar development environment for software engineers.

Quantum Simulators: Microsoft offers quantum simulators that allow users to test and debug their quantum algorithms before running them on actual hardware.

Microsoft's QDK aims to simplify quantum programming and make it accessible to developers with varying levels of experience.

Challenges in Quantum Hardware Development

Despite the promising advancements in quantum hardware, several challenges remain that researchers must address to realize practical quantum computing.

Decoherence and Noise

Decoherence is a fundamental challenge in quantum computing, as it leads to the loss of quantum information over time. Noise from the environment can introduce errors in quantum operations, making it essential to develop error correction techniques and noise mitigation strategies.

Scalability

Scaling up quantum systems while maintaining high fidelity is a significant challenge. As the number of qubits increases, managing interactions between qubits and maintaining coherence becomes increasingly complex. Researchers are actively exploring various architectures and technologies to enable scalable quantum systems.

Integration with Classical Systems

Quantum computing does not operate in isolation; it must integrate with classical systems for data input, output, and processing. Developing effective hybrid models that leverage both quantum and classical computing resources is crucial for practical applications.

Software Development

The development of quantum algorithms requires specialized knowledge of quantum mechanics and programming. Creating user-friendly tools and frameworks that enable a broader audience to engage with quantum computing is essential for fostering innovation in the field.

Quantum hardware and computing platforms are vital components in the quest for practical quantum computing solutions. The diversity of qubit technologies and platforms provides researchers with various tools and approaches for tackling complex problems. Understanding the strengths and limitations of each hardware type is crucial for developing effective quantum algorithms and applications, particularly in fields such as quantum machine learning, optimization, and simulation. As technology advances, overcoming current challenges will pave the way for scalable, efficient quantum computing systems capable of revolutionizing industries and scientific research.

Chapter 12: Quantum Machine Learning Algorithms

Introduction to Quantum Machine Learning Algorithms

Quantum machine learning (QML) algorithms combine the principles of quantum computing with classical machine learning techniques to enhance data processing capabilities and solve complex problems. By leveraging quantum properties such as superposition, entanglement, and interference, QML algorithms can potentially outperform their classical counterparts in various tasks, including classification, regression, clustering, and dimensionality reduction. This chapter provides an in-depth exploration of key quantum machine learning algorithms, their underlying principles, applications, and practical implementations.

Quantum Classification Algorithms

Classification is a fundamental task in machine learning where the goal is to assign labels to input data points based on learned patterns. Quantum classification algorithms leverage quantum mechanics to improve classification accuracy and speed.

Quantum Support Vector Machine (QSVM)

Support Vector Machines (SVMs) are powerful classical algorithms used for classification tasks. The Quantum Support Vector Machine (QSVM) enhances this approach by utilizing quantum computing to find hyperplanes that separate data points more efficiently.

Key Principles:

Kernel Trick: QSVM uses quantum kernels, which enable the mapping of classical data into high-dimensional quantum feature spaces. This allows for more complex decision boundaries compared to classical SVMs.

Quantum Circuit Representation: The quantum kernel is computed using a quantum circuit, facilitating efficient evaluations of similarity between data points.

Implementation:

The QSVM typically involves the following steps:

Data Encoding: Classical data is encoded into quantum states using techniques such as amplitude or angle encoding.

Quantum Kernel Computation: The quantum circuit calculates the quantum kernel matrix based on the encoded data.

SVM Optimization: Classical optimization techniques are used to find the optimal hyperplane in the quantum feature space.

Applications:

QSVMs can be applied in various fields, including image recognition, natural language processing, and bioinformatics, where high-dimensional data representation is crucial.

Quantum Neural Networks (QNNs)

Quantum Neural Networks (QNNs) combine concepts from quantum computing and neural networks to create models capable of learning complex patterns in data. QNNs can represent more intricate relationships than classical neural networks due to their ability to exploit quantum entanglement.

Key Principles:

Quantum Gates as Neurons: In QNNs, quantum gates act as neurons, transforming quantum states through unitary operations.
Entanglement: QNNs can create entangled states that allow for enhanced representation of data, improving learning capabilities.

Implementation:

QNNs generally involve:

Circuit Design: Designing a parameterized quantum circuit that serves as the neural network.
Parameter Optimization: Using classical optimization methods to tune the parameters of the quantum circuit based on training data.
Measurement: Performing measurements on the final quantum state to obtain outputs.

Applications:

QNNs have potential applications in tasks such as classification, regression, and reinforcement learning, making them a versatile tool in quantum machine learning.

Quantum Clustering Algorithms

Clustering aims to group similar data points together based on their features. Quantum clustering algorithms utilize quantum mechanics to enhance clustering performance, particularly in high-dimensional spaces.

Quantum k-Means Clustering

The k-Means algorithm is a classical clustering technique widely used to partition data into kkk distinct groups. Quantum k-Means improves this method by leveraging quantum superposition to accelerate the clustering process.

Key Principles:

Quantum Superposition: By utilizing superposition, quantum k-Means can evaluate multiple cluster centers simultaneously, reducing computation time.

Quantum Distance Measurement: Quantum circuits can be employed to compute distances between data points and cluster centers more efficiently.

Implementation:

The quantum k-Means algorithm typically involves:

Data Encoding: Classical data points are encoded into quantum states.

Cluster Center Initialization: Initial cluster centers are selected, and quantum states are prepared for computation.

Distance Calculation: Quantum circuits are used to calculate distances between data points and cluster centers in superposition.

Update Iterations: The cluster centers are updated based on the assignments, repeating until convergence.

Applications:

Quantum k-Means can be applied in various fields, including market segmentation, image segmentation, and anomaly detection, where efficient clustering is critical.

Quantum Gaussian Mixture Models (QGMM)

Gaussian Mixture Models (GMMs) are probabilistic models used for clustering and density estimation. Quantum Gaussian Mixture Models enhance GMMs by utilizing quantum algorithms to estimate parameters and perform clustering tasks.

Key Principles:

Quantum Probability Amplitudes: QGMMs represent the probability distributions of data points as quantum states, allowing for efficient computation of mixture components.
Entanglement for Correlation: The entangled nature of quantum states allows for capturing correlations among data points that classical GMMs may miss.

Implementation:

The QGMM process typically involves:

State Preparation: Preparing quantum states that represent the Gaussian components of the mixture model.
Parameter Estimation: Using quantum algorithms to estimate the parameters of the Gaussian components.
Clustering Assignment: Performing measurements to assign data points to the appropriate Gaussian component.

Applications:

QGMMs can be utilized in areas such as image processing, speech recognition, and financial modeling, where complex data distributions must be modeled effectively.

Quantum Dimensionality Reduction Algorithms

Dimensionality reduction aims to reduce the number of features in a dataset while preserving important information. Quantum algorithms can significantly enhance this process, allowing for efficient representations of high-dimensional data.

Quantum Principal Component Analysis (QPCA)

Principal Component Analysis (PCA) is a widely used classical technique for dimensionality reduction that identifies the principal components of a dataset. Quantum PCA (QPCA) leverages quantum algorithms to accelerate the computation of principal components.

Key Principles:

Quantum State Representation: QPCA represents data in quantum states, enabling efficient linear algebra operations on large datasets.

Quantum Amplitude Amplification: QPCA uses amplitude amplification techniques to enhance the probability of measuring significant eigenvalues.

Implementation:

The QPCA algorithm typically involves:

Data Encoding: Encoding classical data into quantum states.

Quantum Operations: Implementing quantum operations to compute the covariance matrix and its eigenvalues.

Measurement: Performing measurements to extract the principal components.

Applications:

QPCA can be applied in various domains, including image compression, feature extraction, and exploratory data analysis.

Quantum Singular Value Decomposition (QSVD)

Singular Value Decomposition (SVD) is a powerful technique used in various machine learning and data analysis tasks. Quantum Singular Value Decomposition (QSVD) improves the efficiency of SVD by utilizing quantum circuits to perform the decomposition.

Key Principles:

Quantum Parallelism: QSVD exploits quantum parallelism to compute singular values and vectors more rapidly than classical algorithms.

Quantum State Preparation: QSVD prepares quantum states that represent the singular vectors and values, facilitating efficient processing.

Implementation:

The QSVD process generally involves:

Data Encoding: Classical data is encoded into quantum states.

Quantum Circuit Design: Designing a quantum circuit to perform the SVD operation.

Measurement: Measuring the quantum states to extract singular values and vectors.

Applications:

QSVD can be applied in tasks such as collaborative filtering, image processing, and data compression, making it a valuable tool in quantum machine learning.

Challenges and Limitations of Quantum Machine Learning

Despite the promising potential of quantum machine learning algorithms, several challenges and limitations must be addressed for widespread adoption and practical applications.

Noise and Decoherence

Quantum systems are inherently susceptible to noise and decoherence, which can significantly impact the performance of quantum algorithms. Developing robust quantum error correction techniques is essential to mitigate these effects and ensure reliable results.

Limited Qubit Availability

Currently, quantum hardware is limited in the number of qubits available for computation. This restriction constrains the complexity of quantum algorithms that can be executed, particularly for large-scale problems.

Algorithm Complexity

While quantum algorithms can provide speedups over classical counterparts, the design and implementation of these algorithms can be complex and require specialized knowledge of quantum mechanics and programming.

Integration with Classical Systems

For many applications, quantum machine learning algorithms must be integrated with classical systems. Developing effective hybrid approaches that leverage both quantum and classical resources remains a challenge.

Practical Implementations of Quantum Machine Learning Algorithms

Implementing quantum machine learning algorithms involves using quantum programming frameworks, such as Qiskit and TensorFlow Quantum, to create and execute quantum circuits. Below are examples of implementing quantum algorithms for classification and dimensionality reduction using Qiskit.

Example: Quantum Support Vector Machine in Qiskit

python
Copy code

```
from qiskit import Aer, QuantumCircuit
from qiskit.aer import AerSimulator
from qiskit.utils import QuantumInstance
from qiskit.circuit.library import Z, H, RX
from sklearn.datasets import make_classification
from sklearn.model_selection import train_test_split

# Generate synthetic data
X, y = make_classification(n_samples=100, n_features=4)
```

```python
X_train, X_test, y_train, y_test = train_test_split(X, y,
test_size=0.2)

# Quantum circuit for QSVM
def create_qsvm_circuit(data):
qc = QuantumCircuit(len(data))
for i in range(len(data)):
qc.ry(data[i], i)  # Encode data into quantum state
return qc

# Run the QSVM
quantum_instance                                      =
QuantumInstance(Aer.get_backend('aer_simulator'))
qc = create_qsvm_circuit(X_train
```

Chapter 13: Hybrid Quantum-Classical Approaches

Introduction to Hybrid Quantum-Classical Approaches

Hybrid quantum-classical approaches combine the strengths of quantum computing and classical algorithms to solve complex problems that neither can efficiently tackle alone. These methodologies leverage the unique capabilities of quantum systems, such as quantum superposition and entanglement, while utilizing classical computing resources for tasks that are more straightforward or currently infeasible on quantum hardware. This chapter explores the theoretical foundations, key frameworks, and practical applications of hybrid quantum-classical approaches, providing insights into how they can enhance machine learning and optimization tasks.

Theoretical Foundations of Hybrid Quantum-Classical Approaches

The development of hybrid quantum-classical methods is rooted in the understanding of the strengths and limitations of both quantum and classical systems. Quantum computers excel at specific types of computations, particularly those involving large datasets or complex optimizations, due to their ability to perform parallel processing. However, they also face challenges, such as limited qubit coherence times and error rates, which necessitate the use of classical resources for certain tasks.

Quantum Speedup and Its Limitations

Quantum speedup refers to the potential for quantum algorithms to solve problems more quickly than classical algorithms. This speedup can manifest in various forms, including reduced computation times and the ability to handle larger datasets. However, not all problems benefit from quantum speedup, and for many practical applications, classical algorithms remain highly effective.

Hybrid approaches aim to maximize the advantages of both quantum and classical computing. For instance, while a quantum algorithm may handle the most complex parts of a problem, classical algorithms can efficiently process the simpler components, leading to improved overall performance.

Quantum-Classical Feedback Loops

In hybrid quantum-classical systems, feedback loops between quantum and classical components enable iterative refinement of solutions. For example, in variational quantum algorithms, a quantum circuit is used to evaluate a cost function, and classical optimization techniques are employed to adjust the circuit parameters based on the quantum measurements. This iterative process continues until convergence is achieved, effectively blending the strengths of both paradigms.

Key Frameworks for Hybrid Quantum-Classical Approaches

Several frameworks have been developed to facilitate the implementation of hybrid quantum-classical algorithms. These frameworks provide tools for programming, simulation, and execution on quantum hardware, allowing researchers to explore new algorithms and applications.

Qiskit

Qiskit is an open-source quantum computing framework developed by IBM that enables users to create and run quantum circuits. It supports hybrid algorithms through its various modules, including Qiskit Aer for simulation and Qiskit Ignis for noise mitigation.

Key Features:

Quantum Circuits: Qiskit allows users to construct quantum circuits easily, integrating classical and quantum components.

Classical Optimization: Qiskit offers classical optimization algorithms that can work in tandem with quantum circuits.

Community Support: With a large user base and extensive documentation, Qiskit fosters collaboration and innovation in quantum computing.

PennyLane

PennyLane is a quantum machine learning library that seamlessly integrates with popular machine learning frameworks like TensorFlow and PyTorch. It facilitates the development of hybrid quantum-classical models by allowing users to define quantum circuits and optimize them using classical machine learning techniques.

Key Features:

Differentiable Programming: PennyLane supports automatic differentiation, enabling users to compute gradients of quantum circuits with respect to classical parameters.

Versatility: It can interface with various quantum hardware providers, allowing for flexible execution on different quantum platforms.

Rich Ecosystem: PennyLane's ecosystem includes a wide range of quantum operations and circuits, making it suitable for diverse applications.

TensorFlow Quantum

TensorFlow Quantum (TFQ) is a library designed for hybrid quantum-classical machine learning, allowing researchers to build quantum models within the TensorFlow framework. It combines quantum computations with TensorFlow's powerful machine learning capabilities.

Key Features:

Quantum Layers: TFQ provides quantum layers that can be integrated with classical neural networks, enabling the construction of complex hybrid models.

Simulation and Execution: Users can simulate quantum circuits and execute them on quantum hardware, facilitating experimentation with various architectures.

Support for Quantum Data: TFQ includes tools for handling quantum data, making it easier to apply quantum algorithms to real-world datasets.

Practical Applications of Hybrid Quantum-Classical Approaches

Hybrid quantum-classical methods have demonstrated potential in a variety of applications, particularly in optimization, machine learning, and scientific simulations. Below are some notable use cases.

Quantum Approximate Optimization Algorithm (QAOA)

The Quantum Approximate Optimization Algorithm (QAOA) is a hybrid algorithm designed to solve combinatorial optimization problems. It combines quantum circuits with classical optimization techniques to find approximate solutions efficiently.

Key Principles:

Variational Approach: QAOA uses a parameterized quantum circuit to encode possible solutions to the optimization problem, adjusting the parameters through classical optimization.

Cost Function Evaluation: The quantum circuit is evaluated to determine the cost associated with each solution, guiding the optimization process.

Implementation Steps:

Problem Encoding: The optimization problem is encoded into a cost Hamiltonian.

Quantum Circuit Design: A parameterized quantum circuit is created to represent potential solutions.

Classical Optimization Loop: Classical optimization techniques refine the parameters based on cost evaluations, iterating until convergence.

Applications:

QAOA can be applied to a wide range of optimization problems, including portfolio optimization, scheduling, and circuit design.

Variational Quantum Eigensolver (VQE)

The Variational Quantum Eigensolver (VQE) is a hybrid algorithm used for finding the ground state energy of quantum systems. It combines quantum and classical resources to achieve results that are challenging for classical algorithms.

Key Principles:

Parameterized Quantum States: VQE prepares a parameterized quantum state that approximates the ground state of a Hamiltonian.
Classical Minimization: Classical algorithms optimize the parameters to minimize the energy expectation value.

Implementation Steps:

Hamiltonian Representation: The quantum system's Hamiltonian is expressed in a suitable form.
Circuit Preparation: A quantum circuit is designed to prepare the parameterized state.
Energy Evaluation: The quantum circuit measures the energy expectation value, and classical optimization refines the parameters.

Applications:

VQE is particularly valuable in quantum chemistry for simulating molecular structures and reactions, providing insights into complex chemical systems.

Hybrid Quantum Neural Networks

Hybrid quantum neural networks combine classical neural network architectures with quantum circuits, enabling the development of models that can learn from both quantum and classical data.

Key Principles:

Quantum Circuits as Layers: Quantum circuits can be integrated as layers within classical neural networks, enhancing the model's ability to capture complex patterns.
Classical Training Algorithms: Classical optimization algorithms are used to train the network, adjusting both quantum and classical parameters.

Implementation Steps:

Model Architecture Design: A hybrid architecture is designed, incorporating quantum layers and classical layers.

Training: The model is trained using classical data, leveraging quantum circuits to enhance learning capabilities.

Evaluation: The performance of the hybrid model is evaluated on various tasks.

Applications:

Hybrid quantum neural networks can be applied in areas such as image classification, natural language processing, and generative modeling, where the benefits of both quantum and classical approaches can be realized.

Challenges and Future Directions

While hybrid quantum-classical approaches show promise, several challenges must be addressed to maximize their effectiveness:

Hardware Limitations

Current quantum hardware is limited in qubit count and coherence times, which restricts the complexity of hybrid algorithms. Advances in quantum hardware technology are essential to enable more sophisticated hybrid computations.

Algorithm Development

Designing efficient hybrid algorithms that effectively leverage both quantum and classical components remains a challenge. Ongoing research is needed to explore new algorithms and frameworks that optimize performance.

Integration and Interoperability

Ensuring seamless integration between quantum and classical components is crucial for the successful deployment of hybrid algorithms. Developing standardized interfaces and protocols can facilitate collaboration between different systems.

Scalability

As hybrid approaches gain traction, scalability becomes a critical factor. Researching methods to scale quantum algorithms while maintaining performance and reliability is essential for real-world applications.

Hybrid quantum-classical approaches represent a promising avenue for advancing the field of quantum machine learning and optimization. By leveraging the unique strengths of both quantum and classical systems, these methodologies can tackle complex problems that are currently beyond reach. As research continues to evolve, addressing the challenges associated with hybrid approaches will pave the way for practical applications across various domains, potentially revolutionizing industries and scientific inquiry.

Chapter 14: Quantum Machine Learning in Practice

Introduction to Quantum Machine Learning Applications

Quantum machine learning (QML) is rapidly emerging as a transformative field that combines quantum computing with machine learning techniques. The practical applications of QML span various domains, including finance, healthcare, logistics, and materials science. By harnessing the unique properties of quantum systems, such as superposition and entanglement, QML aims to solve complex problems that are intractable for classical algorithms. This chapter delves into specific case studies and real-world applications of quantum machine learning, illustrating how these techniques are being implemented to drive innovation across industries.

Case Study: Quantum Finance

Portfolio Optimization

One of the most compelling applications of quantum machine learning in finance is portfolio optimization. Traditional portfolio optimization methods rely on classical algorithms to maximize returns while minimizing risks based on historical data. However, as the size of the data and the complexity of the investment landscape increase, classical methods can become computationally prohibitive.

Quantum Approach:

Quantum algorithms, particularly the Quantum Approximate Optimization Algorithm (QAOA), can efficiently solve large-scale optimization problems. By encoding the portfolio optimization problem into a cost function, QAOA can explore potential investment combinations more rapidly than classical methods.

Implementation:

Data Encoding: Financial data, such as asset returns and covariances, is encoded into quantum states.
Quantum Circuit Design: A parameterized circuit is constructed to represent possible portfolio allocations.
Classical Optimization Loop: Classical techniques refine the parameters based on the evaluated cost function, iterating until an optimal portfolio is identified.

Results:

Preliminary studies indicate that quantum portfolio optimization can outperform classical counterparts in terms of speed and the quality of solutions, particularly for large and complex portfolios.

Risk Assessment and Fraud Detection

Quantum machine learning can also enhance risk assessment and fraud detection in financial institutions. Traditional machine learning models rely on historical data and heuristics, which can be insufficient for detecting novel fraud patterns.

Quantum Approach:

By employing Quantum Support Vector Machines (QSVM) or Quantum Neural Networks (QNN), financial institutions can analyze vast datasets and identify anomalies more effectively. These quantum models can capture complex relationships within the data that classical models may overlook.

Implementation:

Data Collection: Transaction data is gathered, including features such as transaction amounts, frequencies, and user behavior.

Model Training: A quantum model is trained on labeled data, allowing it to learn patterns associated with legitimate and fraudulent transactions.

Real-time Monitoring: The model can analyze new transactions in real time, flagging potential fraud cases for further investigation.

Results:

Early implementations have shown promising improvements in the detection rates of fraudulent transactions, demonstrating the potential for quantum machine learning to enhance financial security.

Case Study: Quantum Healthcare

Drug Discovery

In healthcare, quantum machine learning holds the potential to revolutionize drug discovery processes. The search for effective drugs often involves analyzing vast chemical spaces and simulating molecular interactions, tasks that can be computationally intensive.

Quantum Approach:

Quantum algorithms, such as the Variational Quantum Eigensolver (VQE), can simulate molecular structures and interactions more efficiently than classical simulations. By accurately predicting the properties of molecules, researchers can identify promising drug candidates.

Implementation:

Molecular Representation: Molecules are encoded into quantum states, allowing their electronic structures to be modeled.

Simulation: VQE is used to calculate the ground state energies of candidate compounds, guiding the selection of molecules for further testing.

Optimization: The process iterates, refining the parameters to improve the accuracy of predictions.

Results:

Initial studies suggest that quantum simulations can reduce the time and resources needed for drug discovery, potentially accelerating the development of new therapies.

Personalized Medicine

Quantum machine learning can enhance personalized medicine by enabling more accurate predictions of patient responses to treatments based on genetic and clinical data.

Quantum Approach:

Using Quantum Neural Networks (QNN) allows for the modeling of complex relationships in high-dimensional healthcare datasets. These models can help identify optimal treatment plans tailored to individual patient profiles.

Implementation:

Data Aggregation: Patient data, including genetic information, medical history, and treatment outcomes, is collected.

Model Training: A QNN is trained on this data to learn patterns associated with successful treatment outcomes.

Treatment Recommendation: The trained model is used to predict responses to various treatments for new patients.

Results:

Preliminary results indicate that quantum models can achieve higher accuracy in predicting treatment outcomes compared to classical approaches, potentially leading to better patient care.

Case Study: Quantum Logistics and Supply Chain

Route Optimization

In logistics and supply chain management, optimizing delivery routes is crucial for reducing costs and improving efficiency. Traditional optimization techniques can struggle with the complexity of real-world scenarios, especially with numerous variables and constraints.

Quantum Approach:

Quantum algorithms, particularly those based on QAOA, can efficiently explore large solution spaces to identify optimal routes. This is particularly beneficial for complex networks with many delivery points.

Implementation:

Problem Formulation: The logistics problem is formulated as an optimization problem, where the goal is to minimize travel time and costs.

Quantum Circuit Implementation: A quantum circuit representing potential routes is constructed.

Solution Evaluation: The algorithm evaluates the cost of different routes and iteratively refines the solution.

Results:

Early applications of quantum route optimization have demonstrated significant reductions in computational time, allowing for real-time adjustments based on changing conditions.

Inventory Management

Effective inventory management is critical for supply chain efficiency. Traditional methods often rely on historical data and forecasting models that can fail in volatile markets.

Quantum Approach:

By leveraging QML techniques, businesses can improve demand forecasting and optimize inventory levels. Quantum algorithms can analyze patterns in consumer behavior more effectively than classical models.

Implementation:

Data Analysis: Sales data, seasonal trends, and external factors are analyzed using QML models.
Forecasting: Quantum algorithms predict future demand based on historical patterns and trends.
Inventory Optimization: The results inform inventory management strategies, ensuring optimal stock levels.

Results:

Preliminary studies indicate improved accuracy in demand forecasts and more efficient inventory management, leading to reduced waste and costs.

Case Study: Quantum Materials Science

Materials Discovery

Quantum machine learning is particularly promising for materials science, where the discovery of new materials often involves simulating atomic structures and their properties. Traditional computational methods can be limited by computational power.

Quantum Approach:

Using quantum algorithms to simulate molecular structures allows researchers to explore vast chemical spaces rapidly. Quantum simulations can provide insights into properties like conductivity, elasticity, and thermal stability.

Implementation:

Model Setup: Researchers define the properties of materials they wish to investigate.
Quantum Simulation: Algorithms such as VQE simulate the electronic structure of materials, predicting their properties.
Material Selection: The results guide researchers in selecting materials for further experimental validation.

Results:

Initial findings suggest that quantum simulations can accelerate the discovery of novel materials, leading to advancements in fields such as energy storage and electronics.

Optimization of Material Properties

Quantum machine learning can also be applied to optimize the properties of existing materials. This is particularly relevant in industries such as electronics, where material performance is critical.

Quantum Approach:

By employing QML techniques, researchers can model the relationships between material composition and performance outcomes. This enables the identification of optimal formulations for desired properties.

Implementation:

Data Collection: Data on material properties and compositions is gathered.
Model Training: A QML model is trained to predict performance based on different compositions.
Optimization Process: The model iteratively explores variations to identify optimal compositions for target properties.

Results:

Early implementations have shown promise in achieving improved material performance, demonstrating the potential for quantum machine learning to contribute to material innovation.

Quantum machine learning is poised to revolutionize various industries by enabling new applications and improving existing processes. The case studies presented illustrate the transformative potential of QML in finance, healthcare, logistics, and materials science. As quantum technologies continue to advance, the practical implementation of quantum machine learning will likely expand, paving the way for innovative solutions to complex problems. The integration of quantum and classical methods offers exciting possibilities for future research and applications, underscoring the importance of ongoing exploration in this dynamic field.

Chapter 15: Tools and Frameworks for Quantum Machine Learning

Introduction to Quantum Machine Learning Tools

As quantum computing technology evolves, numerous tools and frameworks have emerged to facilitate the development and implementation of quantum machine learning (QML) algorithms. These tools enable researchers and practitioners to harness the power of quantum computing without needing to be experts in quantum mechanics. This chapter explores the most prominent tools and frameworks available for quantum machine learning, highlighting their features, functionalities, and how they can be applied in various QML tasks.

Overview of Quantum Computing Frameworks

Several frameworks have been developed to support the design, simulation, and execution of quantum algorithms, making it easier to integrate quantum techniques into machine learning workflows.

Qiskit

Overview:

Qiskit is an open-source quantum computing framework developed by IBM. It provides a comprehensive suite of tools for quantum programming, simulation, and execution on actual quantum hardware. Qiskit is particularly popular for its user-friendly interface and extensive documentation, making it accessible to beginners and experts alike.

Key Features:

Quantum Circuits: Qiskit allows users to construct quantum circuits easily using Python. Users can design complex circuits by combining quantum gates and measurement operations.

Qiskit Aer: This module provides high-performance simulators for testing and validating quantum algorithms without requiring access to physical quantum hardware.

Qiskit Ignis: This component focuses on error mitigation and characterization, helping users understand and improve the performance of their quantum circuits.

Qiskit Nature: Tailored for quantum applications in chemistry and materials science, this module offers tools for simulating molecular and material properties.

Applications:

Qiskit has been widely used in research and education, with applications in quantum machine learning, quantum chemistry, and optimization problems.

TensorFlow Quantum (TFQ)

Overview:

TensorFlow Quantum is a library designed to facilitate the integration of quantum computing with the TensorFlow machine learning framework. It allows users to create hybrid quantum-classical models that can leverage both quantum and classical data processing.

Key Features:

Quantum Layers: TFQ provides quantum layers that can be incorporated into classical neural networks, enabling the development of complex models that utilize quantum computations.

Automatic Differentiation: TFQ supports automatic differentiation, allowing users to compute gradients of quantum circuits with respect to classical parameters, essential for training quantum models.

Compatibility with TensorFlow: As part of the TensorFlow ecosystem, TFQ seamlessly integrates with existing TensorFlow functionalities, making it easier for machine learning practitioners to adopt quantum techniques.

Applications:

TFQ is particularly suited for applications in quantum machine learning, such as quantum neural networks and hybrid models that combine classical and quantum data.

PennyLane

Overview:

PennyLane is a cross-platform Python library for quantum machine learning, designed to work with various quantum hardware and software frameworks. It emphasizes the integration of quantum circuits with classical machine learning models.

Key Features:

Interoperability: PennyLane supports multiple quantum devices, including IBM Quantum, Google Cirq, and Rigetti Forest, allowing users to run experiments on different platforms.

Quantum Machine Learning: The library includes built-in support for differentiable programming, enabling the optimization of quantum circuits as part of machine learning workflows.

Rich Ecosystem: PennyLane's ecosystem encompasses a variety of quantum operations and circuit designs, facilitating research and development in quantum applications.

Applications:

PennyLane has been utilized in various research projects, particularly those exploring the intersection of quantum computing and machine learning.

Cirq

Overview:

Cirq is an open-source quantum computing framework developed by Google, primarily focused on building and simulating quantum circuits. It is designed for noise-sensitive quantum algorithms and provides tools for both researchers and developers.

Key Features:

Circuit Construction: Cirq offers a flexible API for building quantum circuits, making it easy to define complex quantum operations.

Noise Simulation: The framework includes tools for simulating noise and decoherence, enabling users to test how their quantum algorithms might perform on real hardware.

Integration with TensorFlow: Cirq can be integrated with TensorFlow, allowing users to build hybrid models that leverage both quantum and classical computing resources.

Applications:

Cirq is particularly useful for research in quantum algorithms, quantum error correction, and optimization problems.

Quantum Development Kit (QDK) by Microsoft

Overview:

Microsoft's Quantum Development Kit (QDK) is a comprehensive toolkit designed to facilitate quantum computing development. It includes the Q# programming language, simulators, and integration with Visual Studio.

Key Features:

Q# Language: Q# is a high-level programming language specifically designed for quantum algorithms, making it accessible to developers familiar with classical programming languages.

Quantum Simulators: The QDK includes both local and cloud-based quantum simulators, enabling users to test their quantum programs without physical quantum hardware.

Integration with Classical Languages: The QDK supports integration with Python, enabling users to build hybrid applications that combine classical and quantum computations.

Applications:

The QDK is widely used in research and education, with applications in quantum machine learning, cryptography, and algorithm design.

Developing Quantum Machine Learning Algorithms

Data Encoding Techniques

A crucial step in quantum machine learning is data encoding, where classical data is transformed into a quantum format suitable for processing. Various encoding techniques exist, each with its advantages and trade-offs.

Amplitude Encoding:

Amplitude encoding encodes classical data into the amplitudes of a quantum state. This technique allows for efficient representation of high-dimensional data, as a quantum state can encode exponentially many classical data points.

Angle Encoding:

Angle encoding maps classical data to the angles of quantum gates, facilitating the use of standard quantum operations. This technique is straightforward and can be implemented with existing quantum frameworks.

Basis Encoding:

Basis encoding involves mapping classical data directly onto the basis states of a quantum system. While it is easy to implement, it may require a large number of qubits for high-dimensional data.

Model Training and Optimization

Once the data is encoded into quantum states, the next step is to train quantum models. This typically involves a variational approach, where quantum circuits are optimized to minimize a cost function.

Variational Quantum Algorithms:

Variational algorithms, such as the Variational Quantum Eigensolver (VQE) and Quantum Approximate Optimization Algorithm (QAOA), are commonly used for training quantum machine learning models. These algorithms involve iterative processes where quantum measurements guide classical optimization techniques.

Classical Optimization Techniques:

Common classical optimization techniques include gradient descent, genetic algorithms, and Bayesian optimization. The choice of optimization method can significantly impact the performance of the quantum model.

Evaluation and Performance Metrics

Evaluating the performance of quantum machine learning models is essential to determine their effectiveness and robustness. Various metrics can be employed, depending on the specific application and objectives.

Classification Accuracy:

For classification tasks, metrics such as accuracy, precision, recall, and F1 score are commonly used to assess model performance.

Loss Functions:

Loss functions measure how well the model predictions align with the actual outcomes. In quantum machine learning, specific loss functions tailored to quantum states may be employed.

Benchmarking Against Classical Algorithms:

Comparing quantum models with classical counterparts helps assess the advantages of quantum machine learning. Metrics such as speedup and solution quality are important for this evaluation.

Practical Considerations in Quantum Machine Learning

Hardware Limitations

Current quantum hardware is limited in terms of the number of qubits, coherence times, and gate fidelities. These limitations pose challenges for implementing complex quantum machine learning algorithms on real devices.

Error Mitigation

Quantum errors can arise from various sources, including decoherence and operational inaccuracies. Error mitigation techniques, such as quantum error correction and noise reduction strategies, are essential to improve the reliability of quantum computations.

Scalability

As quantum technologies advance, scalability becomes a critical consideration for the widespread adoption of quantum machine learning. Developing algorithms that can scale effectively while maintaining performance is a key area of ongoing research.

Interdisciplinary Collaboration

Quantum machine learning lies at the intersection of quantum physics, computer science, and machine learning. Collaboration among experts in these fields is vital for advancing the development of effective quantum algorithms and applications.

The tools and frameworks available for quantum machine learning provide a robust foundation for researchers and practitioners to explore the potential of quantum computing in various applications. By leveraging these resources, individuals can develop innovative solutions that capitalize on the unique strengths of quantum algorithms. As quantum technologies continue to evolve, the landscape of quantum machine learning will expand, offering exciting opportunities for exploration and discovery in the years to come.

Chapter 16: Quantum Neural Networks

Introduction to Quantum Neural Networks

Quantum Neural Networks (QNNs) represent a fascinating intersection of quantum computing and artificial intelligence, specifically within the realm of neural networks. By leveraging the principles of quantum mechanics, QNNs aim to enhance the capabilities of traditional neural networks, offering potentially exponential improvements in speed and efficiency for certain tasks. This chapter delves into the theoretical foundations, architecture, and practical applications of quantum neural networks, highlighting how they can reshape the landscape of machine learning.

Theoretical Foundations of Quantum Neural Networks

Quantum Mechanics and Information Processing

At the core of quantum neural networks lies the unique nature of quantum mechanics. Unlike classical bits, which can be either 0 or 1, quantum bits (qubits) can exist in a superposition of states. This characteristic allows QNNs to process information in fundamentally different ways than classical neural networks.

Superposition allows a QNN to represent multiple states simultaneously, providing a form of parallelism that can significantly enhance computational capabilities.

Additionally, **entanglement,** another quantum phenomenon, enables qubits to be correlated in ways that classical bits cannot, further expanding the potential for complex information processing.

Quantum Gates and Operations

Quantum neural networks utilize quantum gates to manipulate qubits, akin to how classical neural networks use activation functions to process inputs. Common quantum gates include:

Hadamard Gate: Creates superposition, allowing a qubit to take on both 0 and 1 states.
CNOT Gate: Generates entanglement between qubits, serving as a fundamental building block for more complex operations.
Pauli Gates: Perform rotations around different axes on the Bloch sphere, enabling a range of transformations.

These gates can be combined to form quantum circuits that serve as the backbone of quantum neural networks.

Architecture of Quantum Neural Networks

Structure of QNNs

The architecture of a quantum neural network can vary widely, but it generally consists of layers of quantum gates arranged in a circuit-like structure. Each layer processes input qubits, transforming them through a series of quantum operations before outputting the results.

Input Layer: The input layer encodes classical data into quantum states, often using techniques such as amplitude encoding or angle encoding.

Hidden Layers: These layers consist of quantum gates that perform operations on the input states, allowing the network to learn complex patterns and relationships.

Output Layer: The output layer decodes the quantum states back into classical data, providing the final predictions or classifications.

Parameterized Quantum Circuits

Parameterized quantum circuits play a crucial role in the training of QNNs. These circuits include adjustable parameters, typically associated with the angles of rotation applied by quantum gates. During training, classical optimization algorithms adjust these parameters to minimize a loss function, enabling the network to learn from data.

Training Process:

Data Encoding: Classical input data is encoded into quantum states using a suitable encoding technique.
Forward Pass: The quantum circuit processes the input states through multiple layers of gates, producing output states.
Measurement: The output states are measured, yielding classical results that can be compared to the true labels.

Backpropagation: Using a classical optimizer, the parameters of the circuit are updated based on the loss calculated from the measured outputs.

Types of QNNs

Various types of quantum neural networks have been proposed, each with unique architectures and training methodologies:

Quantum Boltzmann Machines: These are generative models that utilize quantum mechanics to simulate distributions over data, allowing for efficient sampling.

Quantum Convolutional Neural Networks (QCNNs): These networks extend the principles of convolutional neural networks to quantum circuits, enabling hierarchical feature extraction from quantum data.

Variational Quantum Circuits (VQCs): These circuits serve as universal approximators, capable of representing any continuous function, making them suitable for a wide range of machine learning tasks.

Practical Applications of Quantum Neural Networks

Image Recognition

Quantum neural networks have shown promise in the field of image recognition, where they can leverage their ability to capture complex patterns in high-dimensional data. By encoding pixel values into quantum states, QNNs can learn to classify images effectively.

Implementation Steps:

Data Preparation: Images are preprocessed and encoded into quantum states.
Model Training: A quantum convolutional neural network is trained on the encoded images, adjusting parameters to minimize classification errors.
Evaluation: The model is evaluated on a test set to assess its accuracy and robustness.

Natural Language Processing

In natural language processing (NLP), quantum neural networks can be applied to tasks such as sentiment analysis and language translation. The inherent parallelism of QNNs can significantly speed up processing times for large text corpora.

Implementation Steps:

Text Encoding: Text data is encoded using techniques such as word embeddings, which are then converted into quantum states.
Model Architecture: A quantum recurrent neural network (QRNN) is employed to process sequences of text, capturing dependencies and contextual information.
Training and Evaluation: The model is trained on labeled text data and evaluated on its ability to classify or translate text effectively.

Drug Discovery

In the realm of drug discovery, quantum neural networks can assist in predicting molecular properties and interactions. By simulating the behavior of molecules at the quantum level, QNNs can identify promising drug candidates more efficiently than classical methods.

Implementation Steps:

Molecular Data Encoding: Molecular structures are encoded into quantum states, representing their features and properties.
Model Training: A quantum model is trained on known molecular interactions to learn patterns associated with efficacy and safety.
Prediction: The trained model predicts interactions for new compounds, guiding researchers in the discovery process.

Financial Modeling

Quantum neural networks can also be applied to financial modeling, including risk assessment and algorithmic trading. By analyzing vast amounts of historical data, QNNs can identify trends and anomalies that classical models may miss.

Implementation Steps:

Data Collection: Historical financial data is collected and preprocessed.
Model Development: A QNN is designed to analyze the data, capturing relationships between different financial indicators.

Decision Making: The model outputs predictions that can inform trading strategies or risk management decisions.

Challenges in Quantum Neural Networks

Hardware Limitations

Current quantum hardware is limited in terms of qubit count and fidelity, restricting the complexity of quantum neural networks that can be practically implemented. As quantum technology progresses, these limitations are expected to diminish.

Training Complexity

Training quantum neural networks presents unique challenges, including the need for efficient optimization techniques. The iterative process of adjusting quantum parameters can be computationally intensive and may require significant resources.

Error Rates and Noise

Quantum computations are susceptible to errors due to noise and decoherence. Implementing error mitigation techniques is crucial for ensuring the reliability of quantum neural networks.

Scalability

Scaling quantum neural networks to handle larger datasets and more complex models is an ongoing research challenge. Developing algorithms that maintain performance while increasing scale is essential for broader adoption.

Future Directions for Quantum Neural Networks

Enhanced Algorithms

Continued research into new algorithms and architectures for QNNs will be vital for unlocking their full potential. Hybrid approaches that combine classical and quantum techniques may yield significant improvements in performance.

Integration with Classical Systems

Integrating quantum neural networks with existing classical machine learning systems will facilitate their adoption in real-world applications. Developing seamless interfaces and interoperability between quantum and classical components is crucial.

Advances in Quantum Hardware

As quantum hardware technology advances, the capabilities of quantum neural networks will expand. Improved qubit coherence, increased qubit counts, and enhanced error rates will enable more sophisticated models.

Interdisciplinary Research

Collaborations between experts in quantum physics, computer science, and machine learning will drive innovation in quantum neural networks. Interdisciplinary research is essential for addressing the challenges and exploring the potential of this emerging field.

Quantum neural networks represent a promising frontier in machine learning, leveraging the principles of quantum mechanics to enhance computational capabilities. By integrating QNNs into various applications—from image recognition to drug discovery—researchers can harness their unique strengths to tackle complex problems. As quantum technologies continue to evolve, the future of quantum neural networks looks bright, with the potential to reshape the landscape of artificial intelligence.

Chapter 17: Quantum Reinforcement Learning

Introduction to Quantum Reinforcement Learning

Quantum Reinforcement Learning (QRL) is a cutting-edge area at the intersection of quantum computing and reinforcement learning (RL). Reinforcement learning, a subfield of machine learning, focuses on training agents to make sequential decisions by learning from interactions with an environment. QRL leverages the principles of quantum mechanics to enhance the efficiency and effectiveness of traditional reinforcement learning algorithms. This chapter explores the theoretical underpinnings, architectures, and practical applications of quantum reinforcement learning, highlighting its potential to revolutionize decision-making processes across various domains.

Theoretical Foundations of Quantum Reinforcement Learning

Basics of Reinforcement Learning

Reinforcement learning involves an agent interacting with an environment in discrete time steps. The agent observes the current state of the environment, takes actions based on a policy, and receives rewards as feedback. The goal is to learn an optimal policy that maximizes the cumulative reward over time.

Key Components:

Agent: The learner or decision-maker.
Environment: The external system with which the agent interacts.
State: The current situation of the agent in the environment.
Action: The choices available to the agent.
Reward: Feedback received from the environment, indicating the success of an action.

Quantum Mechanics in Reinforcement Learning

Quantum mechanics introduces unique characteristics, such as superposition and entanglement, which can enhance the capabilities of reinforcement learning algorithms.

Superposition allows quantum agents to explore multiple actions simultaneously, leading to faster convergence toward optimal policies. **Entanglement** can facilitate complex interactions between states, providing richer representations for decision-making.

Quantum States and Operators

In quantum reinforcement learning, classical states are represented by quantum states, and the actions are associated with quantum operators. The dynamics of the system are described using quantum mechanics principles, allowing the agent to maintain and process information in a fundamentally different manner.

Quantum Decision Making

Quantum decision-making frameworks integrate quantum mechanics into the RL paradigm. These frameworks can lead to the development of policies that explore the action space more efficiently, exploiting quantum parallelism to make better decisions.

Architectures of Quantum Reinforcement Learning

Quantum Value Functions

Quantum value functions extend the classical notion of value functions used in RL. Instead of mapping states to real-valued rewards, quantum value functions map states to quantum states, potentially capturing more complex relationships.

Implementation:

State Encoding: Classical states are encoded into quantum states.
Quantum Value Calculation: A quantum circuit processes these states to compute expected rewards, allowing for more nuanced representations of state-action values.

Quantum Policy Gradient Methods

Policy gradient methods are widely used in RL to optimize policies directly. Quantum variants of these methods utilize quantum circuits to represent and optimize policies.

Implementation Steps:

Parameterization: The policy is represented using a parameterized quantum circuit.
Gradient Calculation: Quantum measurements yield rewards that can be used to compute gradients, which guide the optimization process.
Policy Update: Classical optimization techniques adjust the parameters of the quantum circuit based on the calculated gradients.

Quantum Deep Reinforcement Learning

Deep reinforcement learning (DRL) combines deep learning with RL techniques to handle high-dimensional state spaces. Quantum deep reinforcement learning aims to integrate quantum neural networks with DRL frameworks, leveraging the strengths of both domains.

Architecture:

Quantum Neural Network: A quantum neural network processes the state information and generates action probabilities.
Action Selection: Actions are selected based on the output probabilities, allowing for exploration-exploitation strategies.

Hybrid Quantum-Classical Approaches

Hybrid approaches combine quantum and classical components to exploit the advantages of both. In this architecture, quantum circuits can be used to enhance certain aspects of the RL process, while classical algorithms manage other components.

Implementation Steps:

Classical Control: A classical RL algorithm is used to manage exploration and exploitation strategies.
Quantum Enhancement: Quantum circuits are employed to optimize specific components, such as value function approximation or policy updates.

Practical Applications of Quantum Reinforcement Learning

Robotics

Quantum reinforcement learning can be applied to robotics, where agents learn to perform complex tasks in dynamic environments. By leveraging quantum mechanics, robotic agents can process sensory information more efficiently, leading to faster learning and adaptation.

Implementation Steps:

Environment Interaction: Robots interact with their environments, collecting data on states and actions.
QRL Training: A quantum reinforcement learning algorithm is employed to optimize the robot's actions based on received rewards.
Task Performance: The robot's performance improves over time as it learns to maximize cumulative rewards.

Autonomous Vehicles

In the domain of autonomous vehicles, QRL can enhance decision-making processes, particularly in uncertain and dynamic environments. Quantum algorithms can analyze vast amounts of data in real-time, enabling vehicles to make better navigation and control decisions.

Implementation Steps:

Data Collection: Vehicles collect data on their surroundings, including obstacles and traffic patterns.
QRL Algorithm: A quantum reinforcement learning algorithm processes the data, optimizing routes and maneuvers based on reward signals.
Real-time Adaptation: The algorithm allows vehicles to adapt their strategies in response to changing conditions.

Game Playing

Quantum reinforcement learning has shown promise in game-playing scenarios, where agents learn strategies through trial and error. The ability to evaluate multiple actions simultaneously can lead to faster mastery of complex games.

Implementation Steps:

Game Environment: The agent interacts with a simulated game environment, receiving rewards based on its actions.

QRL Training: The quantum reinforcement learning algorithm optimizes the agent's strategy over time, improving its performance in the game.

Evaluation: The trained agent is evaluated against benchmarks to assess its effectiveness.

Resource Management

In resource management scenarios, such as energy distribution and supply chain optimization, QRL can improve decision-making by optimizing resource allocation strategies based on dynamic conditions.

Implementation Steps:

Resource Data: Relevant data on resource availability and demand is collected.

QRL Optimization: A quantum reinforcement learning algorithm optimizes the allocation of resources based on projected needs and reward signals.

Performance Assessment: The effectiveness of the strategy is assessed through simulations or real-world implementations.

Challenges in Quantum Reinforcement Learning

Hardware Limitations

The current state of quantum hardware imposes significant constraints on the implementation of QRL algorithms. Limitations in qubit count, coherence time, and gate fidelity affect the complexity of models that can be deployed.

Training Complexity

Training quantum reinforcement learning models can be resource-intensive and time-consuming. The optimization process may require many iterations and can suffer from high variance in gradient estimates.

Error Rates and Noise

Quantum computations are susceptible to errors due to environmental noise and decoherence. Mitigating these errors is crucial for ensuring reliable performance in QRL applications.

Scalability

As the complexity of environments and tasks increases, scaling quantum reinforcement learning algorithms becomes a challenge. Developing methods that maintain efficiency and effectiveness at scale is essential for broader adoption.

Future Directions for Quantum Reinforcement Learning

Advances in Quantum Hardware

As quantum technology continues to evolve, improvements in hardware capabilities will enable the development of more complex and powerful quantum reinforcement learning algorithms.

Enhanced Algorithms

Research into new quantum algorithms and techniques for reinforcement learning is critical for unlocking the full potential of QRL. Novel approaches may provide significant speedups and efficiency gains over classical methods.

Interdisciplinary Collaboration

Collaboration between quantum physicists, computer scientists, and domain experts will drive innovation in quantum reinforcement learning. Interdisciplinary teams can address the challenges of QRL and explore new applications.

Real-World Applications

As quantum reinforcement learning matures, its adoption in real-world applications across various domains will become more feasible. Success stories in practical implementations will encourage further investment and research in the field.

Quantum reinforcement learning represents an exciting frontier in artificial intelligence, merging the strengths of quantum computing with the adaptive learning capabilities of reinforcement learning. By harnessing quantum principles, QRL has the potential to enhance decision-making processes across diverse applications, from robotics to resource management. As advancements in quantum technology and algorithms continue, the future of quantum reinforcement learning promises significant innovations that could reshape industries and redefine the boundaries of what is possible in AI.

Chapter 18: The Future of Quantum Machine Learning

Introduction to the Future of Quantum Machine Learning

Quantum Machine Learning (QML) represents one of the most promising frontiers in the convergence of quantum computing and artificial intelligence. As quantum technologies evolve, they hold the potential to address complex problems in ways that classical systems cannot. This chapter explores the future of quantum machine learning, examining emerging trends, potential applications, and the challenges that must be overcome to fully realize the benefits of this revolutionary field.

Current State of Quantum Machine Learning

Progress and Developments

As of now, significant strides have been made in the realm of quantum machine learning. Academic research has expanded, and collaborations between tech companies, research institutions, and governments have intensified. Various quantum algorithms have been proposed, tested, and optimized for machine learning tasks. Frameworks such as Qiskit, TensorFlow Quantum, and PennyLane have made it easier for developers to implement QML algorithms.

Practical Implementations

While theoretical advancements are promising, practical implementations of QML remain limited due to hardware constraints. Nonetheless, several pilot projects and experimental applications have emerged, particularly in areas like quantum optimization, classification tasks, and simulation of quantum systems. Companies like IBM, Google, and Microsoft are leading the charge in developing quantum algorithms that are tested on their quantum hardware, demonstrating early applications of QML.

Emerging Trends in Quantum Machine Learning

Increased Focus on Hybrid Models

Hybrid models that combine classical and quantum techniques are gaining traction. These models allow practitioners to leverage the strengths of both approaches, mitigating some of the limitations of current quantum hardware. By using classical algorithms to handle certain aspects of data processing and quantum techniques for specific tasks, researchers are finding pathways to practical QML solutions.

Development of New Quantum Algorithms

As researchers explore the theoretical foundations of QML, new algorithms continue to be developed. Variational quantum algorithms, quantum kernel methods, and quantum clustering algorithms are just a few examples of innovative approaches being investigated. These algorithms aim to solve complex problems more efficiently, offering speedups over classical counterparts.

Interdisciplinary Research

The future of QML will increasingly rely on interdisciplinary collaboration among quantum physicists, computer scientists, statisticians, and domain experts. This collaboration will facilitate a deeper understanding of how quantum principles can be applied to various fields, from healthcare and finance to materials science and logistics.

Growth of Quantum Hardware

Advancements in quantum hardware will play a critical role in the future of QML. As the number of qubits increases, and gate fidelities improve, more complex QML algorithms will become feasible. Quantum error correction techniques will also enhance the reliability of quantum computations, enabling broader applications of QML.

Potential Applications of Quantum Machine Learning

Healthcare and Drug Discovery

One of the most promising applications of QML lies in healthcare and drug discovery. Quantum algorithms can analyze vast datasets of genetic information, leading to more accurate predictions of disease outcomes and the discovery of new drug candidates. The ability to simulate molecular interactions at the quantum level can revolutionize the pharmaceutical industry, making drug development faster and more cost-effective.

Financial Services

In the financial sector, QML can enhance risk assessment, fraud detection, and algorithmic trading. Quantum algorithms can process complex datasets more efficiently, uncovering patterns that classical models may overlook. This capability can lead to better investment strategies and improved risk management.

Climate Modeling and Environmental Science

Quantum machine learning can significantly improve climate modeling and environmental science by processing large datasets from satellite imagery, sensor networks, and climate simulations. Enhanced predictive capabilities can lead to better climate change mitigation strategies and resource management.

Optimization Problems

QML is well-suited for solving optimization problems, such as those found in logistics, supply chain management, and routing. Quantum algorithms can explore vast solution spaces more efficiently, leading to more optimal solutions in less time compared to classical methods.

Challenges Facing Quantum Machine Learning

Hardware Limitations

Despite significant progress, the current state of quantum hardware imposes substantial limitations. Issues such as qubit decoherence, gate errors, and limited qubit connectivity hinder the execution of complex QML algorithms. Addressing these challenges is crucial for the future of QML.

Algorithm Development

While new algorithms are emerging, many existing QML algorithms still require further refinement and optimization. Theoretical work must continue to ensure that quantum algorithms can provide significant advantages over classical methods in real-world applications.

Education and Workforce Development

As QML grows, there is a pressing need for education and workforce development. Training the next generation of researchers and practitioners in both quantum computing and machine learning will be vital for advancing the field. Educational programs, workshops, and resources must evolve to meet this demand.

Ethical Considerations

The integration of QML into various domains raises important ethical considerations. Issues such as data privacy, algorithmic bias, and the societal impact of advanced AI systems must be addressed proactively to ensure that QML is used responsibly and equitably.

The Road Ahead: Strategic Directions

Investment in Research and Development

Ongoing investment in research and development will be essential to unlock the full potential of quantum machine learning. This investment should span both academic institutions and private companies, fostering innovation and collaboration.

Establishing Standards and Best Practices

As the field of QML evolves, establishing standards and best practices will be critical for ensuring reproducibility, interoperability, and ethical considerations. Developing guidelines for QML research, applications, and data management will help shape the future of the field.

Fostering Collaborative Ecosystems

Creating collaborative ecosystems that bring together stakeholders from academia, industry, and government will facilitate the sharing of knowledge and resources. Such collaborations can accelerate the development of QML applications and drive technological advancements.

Public Engagement and Awareness

Increasing public engagement and awareness of quantum technologies and their potential applications is vital for garnering support and understanding. Outreach programs, public lectures, and accessible educational resources can help demystify quantum machine learning and its implications.

The future of quantum machine learning is filled with promise and potential. As quantum technologies advance and the theoretical foundations of QML continue to evolve, the impact of this field will extend across various domains, driving innovation and solving complex challenges. By addressing current limitations, fostering interdisciplinary collaboration, and embracing ethical considerations, the field of quantum machine learning can lead us into a new era of computing, one that harnesses the power of quantum mechanics to enhance our understanding of the world and improve our decision-making processes.